I0807774

Praise for
The Comparison-Free Life

"*The Comparison-Free Life* is a refreshing drink of grace on a world-weary day. Trade your worries, fears, and addiction to comparison for the hope-filled truths Heather Creekmore mines for you. Read this book, and you'll experience the exhale you need, the holy pause that can come at the end of perfectionism. Friend, you are loved—gloriously as you are."

—**Mary DeMuth,** author of *Pray Every Day: 90 Days of Prayer from God's Word*

"For many women, including myself, freedom from comparison has seemed elusive and impossible. Thankfully, Heather Creekmore has written a hopeful, truth-filled guide for us to finally resist and reject the comparison trap once and for all. It is possible to live the comparison-free life, and it is possible to live joyfully according to how God designed us!"

—**Christine Hoover,** author of *With All Your Heart* and *Messy Beautiful Friendship*

"Heather Creekmore continues to open the door through her brilliant writing for women to look deep into the eyes of a Father who adores them. She is candid and authentic, which makes all of the doubts I have seem . . . just fine. This is one of those books that levels the playing the field and invites us to continually look up. A great read for every woman."

—**Jami Amerine,** author of *Sacred Ground, Sticky Floors*

"In my thirty years in mental health, one of the most prevalent issues I've seen in my office has been not truly knowing our identity in Christ. So many look to others and their accomplishments, only to come up short and lacking in the joy Christ came to give us. Too often we spend our efforts trying to be better, and in the end, we just carry around a burden we were not meant to carry. In *The Comparison-Free Life,* Heather Creekmore uses her characteristic humorous style to help us understand how 'the life of comparison is the old nature, not our new nature.' If you've struggled with comparison, constantly trying to be better, then *The Comparison-Free Life* should be on the top of your stack of books to read next!"

—**Michelle Bengtson,** clinical neuropsychologist, international speaker, and author of *Hope Prevails* and *Breaking Anxiety's Grip*

"A must-read for anyone desiring to reclaim rest in a world of #busy. Heather Creekmore is my go-to on the topic of comparison. With candor and honesty, Heather offers women practical truths to help them embrace their uniqueness and walk boldly in the fullness of who they were created to be."

—**Constance Rhodes,** founder of FINDINGbalance and TRUEvoice.co, and author of *The Art of Being: Reflections on the Beauty and the Risk of Embracing Who We Are*

"When it comes to the problem of women comparing themselves to other women, Heather Creekmore's voice is one that I value most highly. Her empathy and compassion combined with her deep faith, piercing insights, and practical approach make her a trustworthy guide for women seeking to escape the trap of constant comparison. The burden of 'comparison' is one we aren't meant to carry, and I'm grateful to Heather for showing the way to a life of joy, peace, and rest."

—**Richella J. Parham,** author of *Mythical Me: Finding Freedom from Constant Comparison*

"Heather has put her finger on the emotional pulse of an overwhelming majority of women today: the inner push to be more and better, and the fear that we're not enough—all measured by the sinister ruler of comparison. Friends, take this journey with Heather to break out of the comparison prison. Joy awaits you; your daughters will thank you; and Jesus will meet you."

—**Cindy Hawks,** lead pastor's wife of Hill Country Bible Church, women's speaker, and Bible teacher

"This book is ahh-mazing. Certain parts gripped my spirit and rocked me to the core. I am changed. I can't wait to re-read it."

—**Nicole Williamson,** founder of REACH and blogger at *My Reckless Faith*

"Outstanding! I felt like I was reading my own story, but Heather's wisdom leaves me with hope for overcoming this burden of comparison by God's unending Grace!"

—**Tammy L.,** grandma, nature-lover, and professor

"Whoa, conviction with humor in one book? Yes, please! As a fellow CDD sufferer, this is a game changer for me and will be added to my annual reading list!"

—**Michelle B.,** caffeine and Texas addict, and dental nerd

"Incredible; real, honest and heartfelt. How it's all brought together from transparency to transformation is mind blowing. There's freedom in truth when we face it."

—**Amy O.,** poet, stationary addict, and work in progress

"With each page, I could feel the release of the burden of comparison Heather lays out a practical path toward off-loading the weight of comparison. And, it's hilarious!"

—**Lisa B.,** loving wife, homeschooling mom, and juggler of all things

"I want to share this book with everyone I know! It speaks straight to the core of the issues, but with kindness, humor, and grace."

—**Melissa V.,** passionate Jesus follower

"A must-read book, full of powerful messages that have taken me through an amazing, life-changing journey. I finally let go of trying to obtain a 'perfect' body and accepted the one I have."

—**Kathryn M.,** practical personal trainer, mom, and grandma

"Like talking with your best friend, Heather shows us how to lay down the burden of comparison and rest in God's beautiful grace."

—**Kristin A.,** work in progress and child of God

"Women everywhere, from all walks of life, need this book in their lives. It's rooted in Scripture with just enough grit and wit thrown in! A must read!"

—**Melissa H.,** teacher, passable seamstress, and girl mom

"Beauty has absolutely been my idol, comparison my trap. I'm grateful this book points out beauty's deceitfulness and turns your thoughts away from obsession and toward Jesus."

—**Whitney K.,** mom, singer, and diet soda addict

"So thoughtful. Truth filled in a way that makes me bolder. I laughed, nodded, spoke out loud and shouted 'amen' a few times. These are GET BETTER truths."

—**Kara O.,** encouragement enthusiast, Christmas fanatic, wife, and mama

"Gone are the days of ruined vacations and un-celebratory celebrations spent comparing and highlighting our faults when we dig in and lean on our Creator. Expertly and eloquently written."

—**Kelley J.,** blogger, comparison causality, and daughter of the King

"Reading this book feels like sitting down with a good friend who is sharing her heart with you. Such wise words on defeating the comparison trap. I highlighted so much!"

—**Dana H.,** wife, mom, writer, and avid reader

"Girl, I'm so glad I'm not the only one! Thank you a million times over for writing this! This 'always searching for better' heart needed you and the truth."

—**Camber M.,** caffeine addict, sunshine lover, and chaos coordinator

"*I love this book!* Especially how it requires honest, critical thinking on my part. The Comparison-Free Action Plans are great for making this a hands-on, interactive book. Definite read!"

—**Shelly J.,** sweet tea-aholic

"I love how Heather shares her heart! Her practical, biblical teaching creates a desire for soul-searching, leading to freedom and contentment found only in Jesus."

—**Amy V.,** coffee drinker, Jesus girl, and learning to rest

The Comparison-Free *Life*

The Comparison-Free Life

How to Stop Comparing & Find Joy, Peace, and Rest

Heather Creekmore

LEAFWOOD
PUBLISHERS
an imprint of Abilene Christian University Press

THE COMPARISON-FREE LIFE

How to Stop Comparing & Find Joy, Peace, and Rest

LEAFWOOD PUBLISHERS
an imprint of Abilene Christian University Press

ISBN: 978-1-68426-353-0 | previously published as *The Burden of Better*, ISBN 978-1-68426-470-4

Printed in the United States of America

Cataloging-in-Publication Data is on file at the Library of Congress, Washington, DC.

Cover design by Ella Roberts | Interior text design by Sandy Armstrong, Strong Design

Leafwood Publishers is an imprint of Abilene Christian University Press
ACU Box 29138, Abilene, Texas 79699

1-877-816-4455
www.leafwoodpublishers.com

25 26 27 28 29 / 8 7 6 5 4 3

To every woman, young or advanced in years, who, through the common act of comparing herself to another woman, has ever felt compelled, pressured, forced, driven, obliged, required, urged, or prompted to be "better."

And, to my little, red-haired girl, Katie.
May every search for satisfaction lead you back to Jesus.

ACKNOWLEDGMENTS

"What! You too? I thought I was the only one." This iconic C. S. Lewis quote aptly apply to the process of writing and publishing a book about comparison. I want to first pay homage to those friends who helped read and edit, and who fearlessly added input about their own personal wrestling with these issues.

Kristi Lewis, Shannan Vester, Natalie Hodge, Jaime Copley, Christine Salinas, Trisha Mugo, Lisa Beegle, April Birtwistle, April Keenan, Jacky Canada, and Mikalah Gaither: Thank you for your helpful input, insights, and encouragement on the content or the cover! I appreciate each of you so much! Erin Kerry: I'm still amazed at your brilliance in coming up with a title! Thanks, friend. Nicolle Neveu and Lauren Terwilliger: Thanks for demonstrating your friendship through the act of helping me "refine" this work. Alyssa Thorpe: Thank you for letting us use the photo of your gorgeous cake. Cindy Hawks: Thank you for your discipleship and for allowing me to cite that amazing truth nugget God gave you. Jill Hagglund and Becca Fee: Thank you for letting me share your grace stories. And to the community of women who've rallied around *Compared to Who?* and engaged in meaningful conversations about comparison struggles on social media or on the blog: Thank you for naming and confronting issues that are sometimes awkward to even admit! I love you all and pray for your freedom, daily.

Special thanks to my incredible husband, Eric, for your unwavering support of my writing career. Your encouragement is steady and your counsel is wise. I love you. Thank you for leading our family and me well. Zach, Katie, Trevor, and Drew: It's an honor to be your mom. I'm so excited to see how God continues to grow and use you. You're covered in his grace and love. Mom and Dad: Thank you for taking us to church, paying all that Christian school tuition, and imparting in me the truth of God's Word. I love you very much and am so grateful for the encouragement and the heritage you've given me. The team at Leafwood: Thank you for all you've done to take this book from idea to shelf. I'm grateful for your persistence and guidance! I'm blessed to work with you.

Above all, I want to thank Jesus, my savior and redeemer. My heart's desire is that these words lead all who read them into a closer relationship with him. Echoing the psalmist, this is my constant prayer: *May the words in this book and the meditations of my heart be pleasing to you, my Lord.*

CONTENTS

Introduction

THE COMPARISON-FREE LIFE

Don't worry. There's no way she felt my gaze. I stood on the balcony, hidden many rows deep, just like my heart of comparison. Since I remembered the chorus from childhood, I didn't need to read the words. Instead, I analyzed her as I sang each line of the worship song.

"God, you're so good."

Are her legs thinner than mine? They might be. Is she wearing heels? That would make them look thinner, of course—that and the dark denim. I wonder how she gets her hair so smooth when she straightens it. That's a cute sweater set she's wearing. I think I used to own something like that. That would have looked better than this dress I have on. I can barely breathe because of this stupid shapewear. She's probably naturally thin and doesn't have to wear suffocating undergarments.

"God, you're so good."

She has such an incredible voice. I wish I was a better singer. I remember leading worship that one time at youth camp. Of course, the mean sound guy told me he turned my mic way down. I guess singing's still not my thing. Why didn't I take voice lessons? Then I could have been a worship leader. She's so in tune with Jesus; I bet she never struggles like I do.

"God, you're so good. You're so good to me."

As I belted out the last line of the song, conviction overwhelmed me. While singing about God's goodness—to me—I was comparing myself to another woman, sizing her up. At church, nonetheless! *Sigh.* I had measured myself against her from every angle—using fictional rulers I'd constructed to assess my own value. Why must I always compare myself to others? Did I truly believe God was good to *me*? Did I even understand all the aspects of his grace? These are the questions I've wrestled for months, years even, on my journey to finding freedom from comparison.

Do you ever find yourself lost in comparison's labyrinth? See if any of this sounds familiar:

- Do you chase the "ers"? I won't name them all for you, but start with *better,* then add—happier, healthier, thinner, stronger, nicer, wealthier, or smarter. I'm sure you can think of more.
- Do you mentally keep a list of goals that seem to promise they'll take your life from drab to fab if you reach them?
- Do you look at old pictures and compare yourself to the "you" that you used to be?
- Do you look at images of other women and compare yourself to the "you" that you long to be?
- Do you know in your *head* that you shouldn't compare yourself to others but struggle to stop your *heart* from doing it?

If you answered yes to any of these questions, then we have a whole lot in common, my friend. But carrying that burden of comparison weighs us down.

Maybe your burden of comparison feels like guilt—you have a list of *shoulds* scrolling through your mind. Or maybe it feels like obsession or drive—unless you get to that goal, you're sure satisfaction will never come. Sometimes the burden of comparison can even look like healthy determination—success comes to those who "work for it." You don't want to be a slacker, after all.

But what if the better we chase is an elusive destination? When we compare ourselves to others, there's really no objective standard of measure, right? *Better* is a comparative adjective. It can only be defined when in relationship to someone or something else. In other words, better only exists when you're comparing.

Comparison-Free Living

Today, I want to invite you to lay down the burden of comparison and try something revolutionary. I call it *comparison-free living.* Though I'm not a doctor, I feel confident writing this prescription: for your best chance at experiencing a life of joy, peace, and rest, you need to live comparison-free.

"Comparison-free? What does that even mean?" one friend asked me.

"Is that even possible?" another friend chimed in. "Sounds unrealistic."

But with Jesus's help, I know you can live free of comparison. On the list of things God will help us accomplish in this life, I firmly believe "stop comparing" ranks high. We miss so much of what God wants for us because we're looking around instead of looking up.

It might seem hard or even impossible to imagine right now. Comparison may be your constant companion. Like the friend who's a bad influence, you know you shouldn't be hanging out, but there's just something about her that captivates you. Or maybe it feels like comparison's stalking you. She's that random person you always encounter at the oddest of places. She's on the other side of the cereal display in the grocery store. Then you run into her again, randomly, at the PTA meeting, and then again at the gym.

Maybe you always meet her at the worst times. Let's say you get invited to a fancy party and spend weeks planning what you're going to wear. Hair done. Perfect shoes. Extra time on the makeup. Your man is impressed and you feel good. Until you walk into that room and realize Comparison came with you. *How'd she get an invite?* Comparison makes sure you notice every woman in the room who looks (in your estimation) better than you. She diligently keeps at it until your confidence deflates and your shoulders slump. *Why did I think this was going to be fun, anyway?* Can you relate?

I graduated from high school before the invention of social media, but I still spent decades battling comparison and body image issues. Comparison has been around since Bible times—just look at Cain and Abel, two dueling brothers. A few chapters later, sisters Rachel and Leah struggle in a grand contest of one-upmanship. Though the struggle of comparison is older than the pyramids, the avenues we can use to compare are now prolific thanks to technology. Within seconds, you can compare your life to just about anyone's. Anywhere. Anytime.

But, friend, to roll over and back float in comparison's tumultuous sea of insecurity would be a tragic mistake—tragic because God has so much planned for you, just as you are. (Well, mostly. He's got some work to do on your sanctification, I'm guessing. He's still working on me, at least.) Please understand that God is not waiting for you to measure up—to get the look, lose the weight, remodel your home, get those extra degrees, earn the promotion, or even take better selfies! God is not worried about how you compare to those around you. He's got a plan and purpose for your life that doesn't depend on her life, or her life, or even hers. . . . God doesn't saddle us with the burden of comparison. He invites us to rest in his best.

No matter what you're most prone to compare—be it the size of your kitchen or the size of your rear end—I hope you'll embark on this journey to a comparison-free life. To start, we'll take a look at why we compare, what comparison really does to us (hint: it's not as harmless as we think), and how we can really stop it in our hearts. Then we'll explore the way out: a path so soaked in grace that once you experience it, you'll forget about chasing "better."

Bring some friends along for the journey. I have a sneaking suspicion they may be struggling in this same area. You can choose to read this book alone. But reading it with a friend or two (or your small group) means you'll have people to process with and accountability after you've finished reading.

A Journey toward Contentment

Years ago, my doctor diagnosed me with Hashimoto's disease. My thyroid numbers changed from "You may consider getting some help" to "You need medication. Always."

But then my doctor paused and uttered those words I hoped I'd never hear: "You really need to be gluten free. You'll feel better if you can cut it out altogether." I kept it together in her office. Politely, I told her I understood and refused nutritional counseling. (Anyone who's been on as many diets as I have has no problem understanding food ingredients and types.) Then I got in my minivan and cried—a sorrowful mourning of gluten's departure from my life. It felt like a death in the family. *Brownies? Warm French bread? Pancakes? Toll House cookies?* Foods containing flour held a special place in my heart.

To make matters worse, I was headed to gluten heaven—Italy—in two weeks. We'd been saving and planning for this tenth-anniversary trip since our wedding. The timing was awful. How could I possibly enjoy Italy without pizza and pasta? Couldn't my thyroid just tough it out a few more weeks?

But God's grace went with me when I ventured into the land of lasagna and linguini days after swearing off gluten. Gluten intolerance is recognized as a disability in Italy (to not be able to eat pizza in Naples *would be* debilitating), so options abound. Gluten-free pizza and pasta, made the Italian way, taste delicious. I didn't feel deprived for a moment.

And, friend, that's really what this book is all about—contentment. When you live a comparison-free life, you no longer see your deprivations as clearly as you see your blessings. Shedding comparison allows you to embrace grace and experience rest, joy, and peace in amazing new ways. You become full of the plenty, not focused on the lack. After tasting the comparison-free life, you'll never want to go back.

Are you ready to take this journey with me? Then pack some sandwiches (gluten-free for me, please) and let's get to it.

Section One

REALITIES OF THE COMPARISON-FILLED LIFE

Chapter One

SWEATING ALL STUFF

Never compare your journey with someone else's.
Your journey is your journey, not a competition.

–Anonymous

Someday I'll write a memoir called *Beautiful Women Don't Sweat.*

Watch for it.

In it, I'll tell the story of Jenny. Her perfectly straight brown hair and bangs framed her face like a child cuddling a kitten. She turned her head, and her hair effortlessly floated with her. And, most importantly, Jenny didn't sweat.

I stood in the girls' locker room, trying to get my bangs to fluff. (And by fluff I mean stand up, precisely curled and poofed, and stay there.) Of course, my ultra-fine hair didn't cooperate. So I used half a bottle of Aqua Net to help the cause. Jenny didn't use hair spray. The year was 1989, but she didn't need it. *It figures.*

We played field hockey together, which meant practices and running and—in my life—all the things that make one's pores ooze salty liquid. If you didn't endure the 80s, let me offer some insight—sweat and Aqua Net don't mix. Jenny? *Sigh*. She looked just as fresh after practice as before. No smeared makeup, no matted and wet hair. Just perfection. Or so I believed.

Jenny was flawless, while I was beauty's backup dancer. Though no one ever said it directly, I knew, deep down, that Jenny and I were in different leagues. In beauty's social stratification, Jenny was a have. I was a have-not. There's a lot I don't remember about high school. But, somehow, still emblazoned on my hippocampus are images of Jenny—beautiful, sweat-free Jenny—and her perfect hair. Constant comparison leaves a mark.

I decided to do a little research to see what comparison actually does to our brains. Turns out, comparison may legitimately stain our brains more than the average memory. Scientists working with monkeys studied their brain and hormonal responses, and they observed how male monkey cortisol levels (their stress hormone) spiked higher when their mates stood near another male monkey. In other words, monkeys feel jealous. Researchers also found heightened activity in two other parts of the brain associated with social pain and bonding.[1]

Science hints that we connect comparison to social rejection in such a way that it *actually* changes the neural pathways in our brains. These changes can completely alter our core beliefs—including how we see ourselves. Because I compared myself to Jenny, my brain received a message as if someone had actually rejected me—or told me I wasn't as pretty as Jenny. Then, like dripping chocolate ice cream on my favorite white blouse, it left a mark on my brain.

I hate stains on clothes. But stains on one's brain, how do they come off? If it leaves a mark every time I compare myself to someone, I can only imagine what a blotchy mess my brain must be.

Of course, I don't think I would have told you I envied Jenny. *Yikes!* That's too strong a word, isn't it? I just admired her and then compared myself to her. All the time. Jealous? *Nah.* That's something different. It's not like I was the evil stepmother in *Snow White*, devising a scheme to take her out so I could be the fairest of them all. *No.* I just wanted to *be* her. Well, not her exactly. Just a "me" version of her. Beautiful, like her. Fit, like her. Sweatless, like her. A sort of "me-her" hybrid.

Jenny graduated a year before me, but I saw her shadow again in college. I'd love to tell you that I matured my way out of comparison by that time, but lying is not helpful. Instead, college provided a grand opportunity for me to realize that there were so many more women I could be comparing myself to. Why limit my life goals to just being like Jenny? Wouldn't I be the "best" me if I found a variety of people with whom to compare myself? Obviously, I needed sweat-proof skin and hair like Jenny's. But maybe my quest for a better me would benefit from additional role models.

Soon, comparison was my normal—a constant companion on good days and bad. She let me swell with self-satisfaction when life went well. Then she'd drag me to the pit and throw dirt at me on the days I felt I didn't measure up.

The Comparison-Filled Life

This morning I went to a new friend's house. It was like being on the set of a home improvement show. Shiplap, dark wood floors, barn doors, and an incredible white kitchen with subway tile. I asked her if Joanna Gaines *actually* came and designed it. (Waco's not that far away; it was possible!) As I soaked in the beauty of her home, I was reminded that becoming an adult didn't cure comparison in the ways I had hoped.

Instead, adulthood and independence have offered even more ways for me to compare. Grades, clothes, and popularity were the sandboxes comparison played in throughout high school and college. Now there are endless "grown-up" ways I can compare myself to other women. Does her husband *really* plan creative date nights? Are her children better behaved than mine? Does she *really* decorate her front porch every holiday? *Ugh!*

While there's no rational reason for me to feel crushed under the weight of not having a perfect home, a *Sports Illustrated* swimsuit model perfect body, or a *Forbes* top-50 perfect career, some weeks I still do. All the striving. All the stress. Comparison's promise of better trapped me on a vertical slip-and-slide, unable to move forward on the path God intended because I was stuck, scaling and slipping. Up and down. See if any of this sounds familiar.

First, I needed a better body. Because everyone knows that you "should" try to look hotter/skinnier/healthier (pick your favorite "er" word) when you are . . . in your twenties, a bride, a newlywed, a new mom, an old mom, a thirty-something, a forty-something, a pastor's wife, a fitness instructor. (Insert whatever stage or age you may have felt pressure to "look better" here, and I think you'll get what I'm saying.)

Second, I had to be the best. *The best at what?* That didn't really matter. If I was doing it, there was no sense in doing it halfway. I had to be the best student, the best employee, the best in my kickboxing class, the best mom, the best wife, the best friend, the best daughter. Now, granted, I didn't come anywhere close to reaching "best" status in most of these areas. (Especially not kickboxing. Enough said.) But with a postcard reading "Commit Yourself to Constant Improvement" stuck to my desk, I knew that the harder I tried, the better I'd get. I could attain "best" status with more effort. *Someday.*

Third, I wanted to feel like I was winning. Because being the best isn't enough unless you know that the best is actually better than all the others. I used to tell my husband that compliments didn't count unless they included superlatives. Rather than, "You are so pretty," I wanted to hear, "You are the prettiest!" *Yes, I was that crazy*. As you may have noticed, most of life is *not* actually a contest where people are named winners and losers. But those of us who wrestle comparison tend to subconsciously see life as that spelling bee (or beauty contest) we never got over losing. (Fourth place in eighth grade. The word was "ricochet." I thought two c's were in the middle. *I will never forget.*)

With this perspective—when every arena feels like a competitive event—life becomes our own personal Olympics. If you want to win a medal, you play the game. Maybe you've competed in some of these specific competitions too.

Cutest dressed at church. Attending second service (i.e., more time in the morning) and having a healthy assortment of outfits to choose from helped me achieve a gold medal finish in this race some weeks.

Best-behaved children at playgroup. You know, that one day when all the *other* people's kids were biting each other and not sharing Goldfish, mine used their manners and shouted, "Love one another!" at the fighting kids. (So, it only happened the one time. I can hang on to that shining parenting moment forever. #stillwinning)

Best wife. I made a dinner he liked. Cleaned up the house. Showered and put on makeup too. Then (wait for it) did the dishes. All without complaining or silently being mad at him for not complimenting me on changing out of workout clothes. This I graded on a curve because I didn't *actually* know what other wives did. But, in my mind at least, I sprinted the equivalent of a four-minute mile in the best wife race.

Most helpful friend. If she had surgery/a baby/death in the family/tough day, I made a homemade meal and dessert and delivered it to their home across town with a smile on my face. No matter what else was on my calendar. So what if I had to pick up takeout for my family and grumped at everyone within earshot because I was on tilt? I fulfilled my role as the nicest friend ever and showed up at your door with my chicken enchilada casserole and gluten-free brownies. *Someone play my anthem, please?*

Cleanest house when company comes over. The baseboards were clean and every sink shined. Well, at least when expecting visitors—only because I spent the last thirty-six hours cleaning, designating certain areas of the house as off-limits, and yelling at my family to keep things sparkling. Of course, when the company arrived, I'd humbly apologize for the place being such a shambles. "I barely had time to clean the floors. . . ." *She shoots and scores! What a win, ladies and gentlemen! What a win!*

I spent so much time competing in my head that I almost lost touch with reality. My boundaries were way out of whack. (It's hard to have good boundaries when you're trying to please everyone.) My soul was parched, my heart was unsure, and my confidence fluctuated more than the winter weather in Texas. (A single week in January can feature snow days and ninety-degree scorchers!) When you live the life of comparison, it's hard to believe that life is not a contest. Everything inside you wants to keep competing so you know where you stand. *Don't fall behind; that feels awful. Keep making progress. Get ahead. It will help you feel good. It'll bring you more love, more affection, more attention, and more admiration.*

Comparison becomes your identity—driving everything you do and say and affecting every decision you make. But here's the truth: a life stuck in comparison is an existence of both burden and struggle, with no redemption. You always need to do more, have more, *be* more. Comparison captures us in its prison—trying to meet the impossible and ever-changing standard of better. You can't be fully present in the life God designed for you when you constantly wonder what life would be like if it were more like hers.

Expensive Watches

I recently watched a video where a man explained why people buy expensive watches. To me, a $200 watch sounds a tad excessive. But there are some who wear—on their wrists—timepieces that cost ten times the worth of my minivan. The speaker offered an incredible explanation for why people wear such fancy watches: It's because they can't take their yachts out to dinner with them. *Of course! Wait, what?*

Expensive watches, he explained, are the culmination of the comparison battle. At median income levels, people compete with houses and cars. At the next higher bracket, they compete with better homes and better cars. But eventually you reach a point where you jockey for status by owning the best yacht or biggest island. Since you can't carry those wealth symbols around, you buy a $100,000 watch.

Interesting, but sad. Right? How hollow that must feel. Even the wealthiest of the wealthy don't escape the comparison game—the satisfaction of "winning" still eludes them. It seems there's no actual top rung to comparison's ladder. Sure, you may never have shopped for a Rolex because you couldn't carry your yacht around. But, friend, the same principles that apply to the comparison of wealth apply to every area in which we compare ourselves. When we compare, there's no winner—only losers trapped in a hollow life of comparison.

Trapped in the Middle

I'm sitting at my desk watching a wasp that somehow got stuck between the screen and the window. He keeps trying to fly full speed into the screen to get back out to the yard but can't break through. Then he buzzes over to the glass to try to break free into our home. Back and forth he goes, buzzing around and searching for any opening. Though I'm happy he can't get in, I can only imagine the frustration going on in his bug mind. He sees vast pictures of freedom on each side, yet he stays trapped in the middle.

Comparison traps us in the same way, distracting us from fully living. Instead of experiencing joy and rest, we stay stuck, buzzing at the window. We see life but never know contentment. Sadly, too many are convinced there's no other way. I watched a wonderful Christian woman on YouTube share this very idea with her million followers. Comparison, she lamented, could not be controlled. Our best hope is to know how to console ourselves after we do it.

I disagree. Yes, comparison may be a habit—but habits can be broken. Yes, comparison may come naturally—but that doesn't mean we bow to her demands. Comparison isn't an undefeatable beast. She's more like a scary shadow on the wall. Once you point enough light at her, she disappears.

Whose Ugly Is Ugliest?

So how do you shine the light on comparison and make her go away? This seems to be a hot topic for Internet memes. Maybe you've even reposted them. One popular picture quote is attributed to Steven Furtick: "The reason we struggle with insecurity is because we compare our behind the scenes with everyone else's highlight reel." That's a fine statement. There's some truth there. Too often, we do compare their sparkle to our shambles. In this Facebook age, our friend's perfect family picture pops up on the day we didn't have time to shower or get the kids out of their pajamas. We fight with our spouse, then get on Instagram and see a friend's "so romantic" date night. But here's my problem with this as a proposed remedy for comparison: What if my ugly really *is* uglier than your ugly?

- What if their marriage fight is over toothpaste and yours is over infidelity?

- What if their parenting problems are too many video games while yours involve serious rebellion?
- What if she battles the scale for ten pounds while you're fighting to lose a hundred?

I wonder if this quote instructs us to compare our worst with someone else's worst, instead of quitting comparison altogether. How do we stop comparing when we really are struggling? Pretty platitudes can't answer this question.

Then there's another way some attack the comparison problem: tell people to focus inward. We instruct our teenage girls not to compare themselves with the magazine covers because it's what's on the inside that counts. We encourage everyone to "be their best selves" and to only compare where *you* are today with where *you* were yesterday. That's not awful advice, for some. But I know many women who are caught in a prison of comparing who they are today with who they were ten years ago. How can this advice free them? Let's be honest. Does anyone ever actually feel better after hearing, "It's what's on the inside that counts"?

Instead of defeating the beast, pithy quotes only put comparison on a leash to keep it from running wild. If we treat comparison as a pet to be tamed instead of a pest to be eliminated, we sidestep real spiritual issues that require our attention. When our hearts wonder, "Is it *really* okay that I'm not like her?" the only truly satisfying answers come from the gospel. Comparison isn't an external issue focused on who we are or the abundance of our possessions. Comparison's quest for better is an issue of the heart.

The Beast of Better

If you think about it, comparison always presents itself as an issue best resolved through improvement. If I could just *have* a better body, home, children, clothing, car, career, marriage, you name it . . . then I would stop comparing. If I could just get *this* part of my life right, if I knew I was succeeding in some part of it, *then* I'd stop. If everything could just *be* a little better, then I could find rest. Comparison's prison is an if-then paradox. Our joy, our rest, our happiness, and our peace all depend on meeting our goals, getting what we desire, or, in the worst cases, capturing the ever-elusive beast of better. This is when better becomes a burden. A massive burden!

"It's not about you; it's about *me*," we convince ourselves. "Comparison is not a *big* deal," we reason. "It's necessary for my self-improvement," we rationalize. My comparison doesn't actually hurt anyone. Does it? I'm afraid the Bible disagrees. It tells us not to size up other people (James 2:1). The apostle Paul tells us in 2 Corinthians 10 that comparing ourselves is foolish. When we become winners at the comparison game, we puff up with pride. But pride hurts our relationships by causing both division and strife (Prov. 13:10; 1 Cor. 4:6–7). When we become losers in the comparison game, we are filled with envy, doubt, jealousy, and even lust. That's not healthy for anyone either.

I'm guilty too, so please don't hear any condemnation in that last paragraph. The anthem of "do better like her" beats in my head too often. My heart's intent is to lift you up, not tear you down. Yes, I want us to clearly see what happens when we wear that burden of comparison. But know even the toughest parts of this journey will be accompanied by a symphony of grace because that's the only tune that will carry us out of comparison's cacophony.

I write about life in the land of comparison because I spent so much time there that they forced me to register my car. I didn't understand grace or what it could be like to live comparison-free. But daily I'm learning to surrender my proclivity to chase better—and daily I ask God to help me learn to rest in him.

Like an Instagram filter, a greater understanding of God's grace tints and clarifies the way we view the world and our place in it. That filter of grace helps us see every event, every struggle, and every triumph differently. Likewise, the filter of gratitude can help us actually change the way our brains are wired, wiping off those stains comparison left, so that we spend less time comparing and more time savoring the days we have.

Comparison isn't something you simply decide to get over. It's not a life stage you grow out of (ask some of my blog readers who qualify for senior discounts at department stores); nor is it a trivial habit you can choose to write off as "no big deal." Every minute you spend comparing is time stolen from your pursuit of God's plans for you.

Your Journey Begins

In the first part of this book, we'll look at some of the not-so-obvious reasons we compare ourselves to others and how the often quoted "stealing of our joy" may be one of comparison's milder consequences. I refer to these as the "me reasons" to stop comparing.

Then we'll look at the "He reasons" we should give comparison the boot. In Section Two, we'll explore some of the resources God has given us for combating comparison effectively—namely the four different types of grace. We'll look at how to filter our view of life through each of grace's different manifestations. When we understand all that we already have through Christ, we can more confidently lay down that burden of comparison.

In the final section, we'll look at how to practice grace, gratitude, and contentment so we can stop viewing our lives through the lens of comparison and instead experience the peace, joy, and rest God intends us to have as his children.

Portions of this book were written in our minivan. My fighter-pilot-turned-pastor husband was able to take a sabbatical before the start of our next ministry opportunity, so we hit the road. Our journey took us through the desert, to the Grand Canyon, to both coasts, and home to Texas again. Some days—like our whale-watching trip in Southern California—have been amazing. Others—like when half the family burned with fever but we kept driving—were not as magical.

As you start your own journey toward a comparison-free life, you may experience different terrains too. You may feel amped up, ready to stop comparing right now! But in a few days, that temptation to compare may come back even stronger. Let me encourage you: that's normal. Have you ever tried to give up sugar? Then you may know how by day three, gummy bears and Oreos are all you can think about. There are similarities. But stick with it. Throughout the course of this book, you're going to gain the tools you need to overcome the temptation to compare. Work through the material, one chapter at a time—and don't skip those journaling exercises and the memory verses at the end of each chapter. They'll help a lot. When comparison entices you with its empty promises, you need to be equipped with Scripture to answer it back.

The longing for better can either leave us glaring at our reflections in futility or growing in maturity as Christians. Discovering true purpose and freedom in Christ has transformed every part of me, and it can do the same for you. You *can* stop comparing, and trust me, once you get a taste of the comparison-free life, you'll never want to go back.

Takeaway

Comparison's contest doesn't have any winners. Instead of searching for a higher rung on comparison's ladder, it's time to hop off.

Comparison-Free Life Action Plan

Read 2 Corinthians 10. What does this passage teach us about winning our battles against struggles like comparison? What else do you notice in this passage that could apply to comparison?

1. In which areas of your life do you find yourself most likely to compare?

2. Can you think of any examples of how comparison has trapped you or kept you from doing something you wanted to do or dreamt of doing?

3. How have you fought the "elusive beast of better"? In what ways have you felt the pressure of the if/then paradox? (If you did this, got this, looked like this, *then* your life would be better in this way.)

4. What area of comparison might be the most difficult for you to give up?

5. Do you believe that comparison could be a spiritual issue instead of anything related to your possessions, success, looks, and so on?

Memory Verse: "For you, O Lord, are my hope, my trust, O Lord, from my youth" (Ps. 71:5).

Lord, help me as I begin this journey toward a comparison-free life. Open my eyes to the ways I've allowed comparison to distract me from your purpose. Show me your truth in a personal way as I take this journey. Help me desire more of you and less of me. Amen.

Chapter Two

WANTED—A BETTER LIFE

Your time is limited, so don't waste it living someone else's life.

–Steve Jobs

This morning I cracked open a new book on the Enneagram, a now-popular way to categorize personality types. (I'm a sucker for these types of tests. Though I'm careful not to yield them too much credence, they can be entertaining.) The basic concept touts that we all have an essence—a way of being that is natural to us. There are nine types, each driven by certain fears and prone to certain strengths and weaknesses. I'm a seven. Today, after what I learned about my type, I'm questioning many of my life decisions.

Sevens frequently struggle with gluttony. *Guilty!* Sevens are prone to addictions and overindulgence. (I always knew that I shouldn't drink alcohol for this reason. Crying shame I never felt that conviction about chocolate.) My type craves fun, excitement, new experiences, and adventure. *Yes! Yes! Double yes!* I hate to do the same thing for two days in a row (unless it's sitting on the beach). My husband says I come from "fun country."

Sevens don't like to make decisions until they've experienced all their options. One illustration talked about how sevens can't choose their favorite flavor of ice cream—they prefer scoops of several different flavors. I laughed. Just yesterday, I ran in to Aldi to purchase one half-gallon and came out with two. *How could we possibly only offer one flavor to our children?* That felt wrong. Apparently, sevens are also prone to hoarding. (I chose that word.) The book described it as a fear of lack. *Gasp! They know me so well!* If I'm making dinner for a group of fifteen, I will make forty servings before ever calculating what it would take to make just enough. *What if we ran out? What if someone didn't get a plateful? What if there are no leftovers?* I can't really think of anything worse than that. #noleftovers #notwinning

And sevens, generally, just want a better life. We're on a quest to answer a voice that tells us that things could be better if our experiences were more fabulous. *Alexa, cue my "better life" playlist, please.* Sometimes I believe it's my next vacation that will make me happy. It's the next chocolate in the box that will satisfy me (especially if it's salted caramel). The next bargain rack outfit I purchase . . . the next home improvement I make . . . the next book I write. . . . Only, it doesn't. And I eat that entire box of chocolates before I come to my senses (while nursing a mighty stomachache).

Even if you're not an Enneagram seven, I have a hunch you've probably also searched for ways to make your life better. The ones seek perfection, while the threes seek a better résumé. Even the twos long to support others in "better" ways. We all find ourselves striving for the elusive better sometimes, right? It's programmed into us from culture, media, and marketing. I doubt we're even conscious of it most of the time. But is it okay?

Is It Wrong to Want a Better Life?

So what's wrong with wanting life to be richer, fuller, more satisfying? Isn't comparison really just our hearts longing for more?

At face value, nothing's wrong with wanting life to be better. God wants us to dream and grow. Relationships that are cultivated offer more satisfaction. Life feels invigorating when we're engaged and serving. God placed within us a healthy and holy dissatisfaction with the status quo. Many of these longings are good. But too often, we forget that this life is not the main event. Yes, it's okay to long for better—as long as you're defining it God's way.

I speak on body image and tell my story to women all over the country. I talk about believing that a "perfect" body would give me all I ever wanted out of life. In reality, for that week or so that I was able to zip up a small size, misery never subsided. Intellectually, I knew that I was as thin as I'd ever be. I was an aerobics instructor—the one title I thought would validate me as fit enough. Yet my smaller body didn't make me as happy. I still felt uncertain. I look at the pictures from that time and am shocked because I only remember feeling dissatisfied with my appearance. Every time I share this story, a few women come up to me and tell me they experienced the same thing. They got the body they always believed they wanted, only to find themselves just as miserable (if not more miserable), frustrated, and hopeless.

We know this to be true in other areas of life too. Look at all the crazy stories of people winning the lottery—only to wind up in greater despair and depression than they ever faced before wealth. Some studies even show that lottery winners are less happy than recently paralyzed accident victims.[1] Shocking, right? Tremendously successful celebrities or musicians reach the top of their game and then struggle with depression or even suicide. Actor and comedian Jim Carrey said it this way: "I think everybody should get rich and famous and do everything they ever dreamed of so they can see that it's not the answer."

It's a tough truth, but it collides head on with our comparison issues, doesn't it?

- The best house won't make you happy.
- The best husband won't keep you content.
- The best body won't last forever (or bring you the deep and meaningful love you hope it will).
- The best (fill in the blank with whatever you are dreaming of) won't satisfy.

God created us with longing. *Yes*. But he created us so that longing would only be satisfied in one place—in him. Trying to satisfy it with anyone or anything else always falls flatter than my bangs after gym class in the 1980s.

There is a healthy way to crave a better life—we should crave more of Jesus, more of his grace and growth. (We'll explore all of this in future chapters.) But, if you're like me, your struggle with comparison is more about looking for a better life here and now. Too often, we determine what qualifies as "better" through the lens of comparison instead of through the filters of grace and gratitude.

The Hidden Problem

I'm addicted to the *Greatest Showman* soundtrack. Still. Years later. If you haven't seen the 2017 musical, I'll warn you right now: you'll probably download the soundtrack before you get the Blu-ray ejected.

In one scene, P. T. Barnum tries to convince a young man from the upper crust named Phillip Carlyle to join the circus management. Barnum and Carlyle sing a song called "The Other Side," in which the elder Barnum tells a young Carlyle that he can set him free from the stifling expectations of his social class. Carlyle's response: "I quite enjoy the life you say I'm trapped in." He says he doesn't need to see the other side; he's not in a cage. Through an ingenious musical negotiation, eventually Carlyle changes his response. Deep down, he knows his current life lacks joy.

We do a lot of "playing the part" in our daily lives. Don't we? It's easy to get caught up in everything from culture's definition of what "should be" to our friend's Instagram post that shouts how we're missing out. We read self-improvement books so we can hustle harder or eradicate bad habits. Our hearts ache with longing. *I just want a better life! Can I trade this one in for a new one?*

The first step in finding freedom (from anything, really) is admitting we have a comparison problem. *Yikes.* But, friend, denying it keeps us stuck. There's a reason twelve-step programs start with confession. But let's dig a little deeper. What if we could admit that most of our comparison struggles are really struggles with issues like identity, value, and acceptance? Instead of comparing ourselves to others because we crave a better life, I wonder if, instead, we actually compare ourselves to others for these three reasons:

- We want to know if we're normal.
- We want to know if we're acceptable.
- We want to know if we're worthy to be loved.

Am I Normal?

Facebook provides an amazing world of things, both useful and useless. One particular evening its more useless offerings intrigued me.

It was Saturday night (a lonely night for many pastors' wives) and a mom friend of mine—procrastinating on finishing homework for a college course—was taking quizzes. Not quizzes for her class, of course. But the kind of quizzes where you find out what animal you are most like or what color best captures your personality. *Thank you, BuzzFeed.* As is often the case with these social media boondoggles, when you take the quiz, you have to invite friends to reveal your answers. My feed filled up with invitations to take the quizzes too.

The first one went well. Apparently, I should live in New York City. I liked that answer. I walk fast, talk fast, and wear black, and even though I'm trying to wear brighter clothes and bigger earrings so I look more like a Texan, I'll always be an East Coast girl deep down.

But when I finished the next one, my smooth ride through quiz-land ended. The directions: answer questions and let the quiz see your profile picture so the magic machine can tell you which celebrity you resemble most. *Innocent enough.* My cute friend got Reese Witherspoon—a great match for her. I pressed "like" and felt excited to see my results. (Completely shallow. Yes, I know.) *I wonder who I'll get?* My excitement quickly turned to dismay as the program proceeded to show me that my celebrity twin was . . . a man! Actually, *man* is an overstatement. It was some Justin Bieber contemporary whom I'd never even heard of! I wish (really, I do) I were joking. I changed my Facebook profile picture immediately. *Obviously it wasn't a good likeness.* Because I love being disappointed, I tried it again. (Apparently I have too much free time.) Same results. *You've got to be kidding me!*

My dear friend Deena tells me that I look like Valerie Bertinelli—the *One Day at a Time* star who now has her own cooking show. I think she means it as a compliment. She always kindly adds the disclaimer, "a younger Valerie." *Okay, I may be able to see some resemblance.* So why, oh why, couldn't this random Internet program come up with a result like that? Or why not lie and say I look like Carrie Underwood or Jennifer Garner? *Just make me feel good so I'll keep taking your stupid quizzes.* Frustrated and aggravated, I logged off. I'm traumatized, you understand. Since then, I avoid every Facebook quiz link.

Why do we love quizzes so much? What's so enticing about them? If you stop and think about it, it's bizarre. Why would we want some stranger to tell us who we are based on arbitrary questions? Odd, right? Yet we open the quiz and cruise through every multiple-choice question like brainy kids taking the SAT, number-two pencils sharpened. *Which should I pick? Which is most like me? So much is riding on this!* Then we feel discouraged when none of the answers seem to fit. *Uh, oh. This is going to impact my results. I don't match any of these! Help!* Finally, with great anticipation, we flip to the answer key. There it is: the wisdom we seek. Do we sleep better knowing what type of playground mom we are or which Disney princess we most resemble?

We're intelligent women. How does it make sense that we would even care about some silly quiz and its preprogrammed answers?

I asked some friends on Facebook why they thought we were drawn to quizzes. "They're fun," some responded. "They're an amusement, a good distraction from laundry or cooking dinner." But, friends, it's more than that. Quizzes tap into some of our deepest desires. The exercise of looking through answers, identifying with certain statements, and then finding out our label or category helps us feel something—it helps us feel normal because we have something with which to compare ourselves.

Normal is not a big word, but it's a loaded one. For years, I thought I knew how to define it. Then I grew up and realized that my normal was not my roommate's normal or my bosses' normal or my friends' normal, and it was most certainly not my husband's normal. There's a big part of me that wants this so badly. I want to be normal. I want to know that I'm okay. Do you ever feel that way? And what happens when I don't feel normal? Things fall apart. One of the biggest lies Satan tells is that we're the *only* one who feels what we're feeling or experiences what we're experiencing. The enemy's trick is to convince us that we *aren't* normal. Then we frantically compare ourselves to others to see if he's telling the truth.

And that's where quizzes come in. We look to quizzes, personality tests, and all sorts of typecasting exercises to affirm us. When we easily find the right box to check, our spirit sings, "Oh yes, that's me! Hooray! I'm okay." Subconsciously, we recognize that our "type" made the answer key. If someone else can check the same answers and get the same results, we're not odd. We take comfort in knowing others are out there who are just as compulsive or carefree; otherwise, they wouldn't have their own space on the answer key. Somewhere out there, someone else sees things our way. That feels good to know.

But no quiz can aptly affirm us. Our comfort must come from knowing the one who knit us together in our mother's womb and in whose image we were made. Likewise, comparison can't definitively answer the "Am I normal?" question. Compared to one group, you may be normal. Compared to another—you're a giraffe in the chicken coop. Attempting to quell this question of the heart by looking around us only amplifies our insecurity.

Normal feels like a solid place to rest our identity. If we're "normal," then we're "okay" and acceptable—maybe we're not at the top of the heap, but at least we're not staring up from the bottom. But normal is like that cozy sweatshirt you'd never wear outside of the house. You throw it on to keep you warm inside, but it's not nice enough to wear out to dinner. God wants more than just BuzzFeed's definition of normal for his children. He doesn't want our identities tied to our ability to meet a cultural average. Why settle for normal when God calls us to stand out? Why find confidence in the shifting sands of our culture's definition of normal when Christ says we can rest our identities securely in him?

Am I Acceptable?

During my junior year at Messiah College, my four roommates and I were interrupted during our studying (read: chatting) by abnormally loud music coming from the apartment below. It didn't take long for us to realize the boys downstairs weren't having some sort of jam session; they were "serenading" us. As a shout-out to the girls in apartment 303C, they set the volume to maximum so we could hear the song too. *How sweet!* Except for one detail. Their song of choice was "Fat Bottomed Girls."

My roommates found this hilarious. They laughed and opened the windows. To play along, they started dancing and even shoved pillows into their backsides to "up" the fun. I did not dance. I did not put a pillow in the back of my jeans. I can't remember exactly what I did, but I know how I felt. As my friends danced and shook their tail feathers, my soul flooded with shame. I assumed I was the reason they chose that fat-bottomed song. (My fluctuating weight proved to be one of my biggest challenges during college.)

Frozen with a nervous smile, I stood there watching. Soon, those voices inside my head became louder than the music. Shame began its bludgeoning: "You should be thinner! What size are those jeans you're wearing right now? *Jumbo?* Of course they'd dedicate *that* song to you because *you* aren't beautiful. You're ugly. Beautiful women are serenaded with love ballads. Fat and undesirable women like you are mocked with vintage Queen songs. You'll never find love. This is what all men think of you."

That wasn't the end of shame's scorn. It kept going. Truth is, shame has reminded me of this incident for years. Make that decades. Shame tells us we're not accepted. I recently heard of a young woman who told her pastor's wife she stopped coming to church because she was too fat. *She barely wore a size eight.* Shame came in the garden when Adam and Eve took the fruit from the tree of the knowledge of good and evil. I love how one organization, the Bible Project, defines what happened at that moment: Adam and Eve had to choose whether they would accept God's definition of what was good and evil or whether they would they seize autonomy and define for themselves what was good and evil. Think about it like this: Adam and Eve already had perfect, but Satan convinced them to sin so they could find "better." When they chose to chase better over accepting God's best, they not only changed the trajectory of mankind, but they also experienced something they had never felt before—shame (Gen. 3:7).

Shame enslaves us to comparison. We wonder if we looked more like her or acted more like her, would shame leave us alone? The answer is no. Shame doesn't work that way. Instead, shame turns us into shamers. Not out loud, of course. Most of us never audibly mutter those ugly thoughts we think in our heads. But shame—matched with a longing for acceptance—propels us to compulsive comparison. *Did she honestly just say that to her kids? I'm nicer than she is—probably a better mom too. Has she gained weight? I wonder if I'm smaller than she is now.* In the darkness of our minds, shame traps us on the "how am I compared to you" scale.

Our acceptability can never be definitively determined through comparison. Monitoring the successes and shortcomings of others to determine our own value puts us in an unhealthy place—one that Jesus died to rescue us from!

Am I Worthy of Love?

Fast-forward a few years. I was twenty years old, living with four roommates in a Washington, D.C., townhouse. Each morning, I walked four blocks to my job in a congressman's office on Capitol Hill. And each evening as I returned home, after mentally sorting through the events of the day and what frozen entree I'd make myself for dinner, I asked myself some variation of this question: Will anyone ever love me?

Sure, I knew my parents loved me. My friends? They probably did too. But it felt like real love—the love that would come from some man who would bring me flowers and grin from ear to ear at the sight of me in a pretty dress—was too difficult to find. I wondered if I was even worthy of love.

Today, we don't have to wonder about love anymore—we just Google. I searched "What makes someone worthy of love?" minutes ago and found 280 million entries. (Apparently, others have wrestled with this question.) One author's solution intrigued me. *Psychology Today*'s Dr. Saul Levine believes that what makes a person feel worthy of love is being, belonging, believing, and benevolence. You'll know you deserve love when you check each of these boxes.[2]

But there's nothing tangible about any of those criteria! *Yikes!* For chronic comparers or perfectionists driven to always do better—how can we know when we've done enough? Could I have been more kind or generous? *Always.* Could I have more friends and social connections? *Probably.* Could I do better in my walk with God? *Certainly.* How comfortable am I in my own skin? *Well, better than last year or last decade—but don't ask me to model swimsuits. Okay?*

If what makes us worthy of love ties to some sort of self-actualized acceptance of our humanity, we'll stay stuck on comparison's treadmill.

The Better Life Express

Books about how to have a better life top best-seller lists. Why have a meh life when marvelous is possible?

Accordingly, there are an unlimited number of little tweaks you could make that will somehow better your life. You can budget to improve your financial situation or walk to improve your health. You can wake up or go to bed earlier, grow your own vegetables, or only buy organic produce. This ever-elusive state of better is always just a change or two away. None of these adjustments are inherently bad. The challenge comes when the comparison beast turns us into better-seekers instead of Jesus-seekers. Slowly we turn our hearts away from the source of all that is good and toward the illusion of self-made satisfaction. When we question our worthiness, belonging, and normalcy and answer with data gleaned from comparison, we never find contentment.

Perhaps we don't long to be billionaires or supermodels. But we can still get stuck believing that just a little more money or beauty will be enough. If we just had as much as they do, then we could rest.

While Jesus says all who seek will find, comparison's con keeps you seeking and never finding—separated, isolated, and filled with doubt (Matt. 7:7). For this reason, the con must be exposed.

Takeaway

At some level, we all long for a better life, but self-improvement or obtaining all that we desire won't solve our comparison challenges. Too often we look to comparison to answer questions of our hearts, such as, "Am I normal?," "Am I acceptable?," and "Am I worthy of love?" Though it's easy to stay stuck on the "Better Life Express," we must expose comparison's con to find contentment.

Comparison-Free Life Action Plan

Read Romans 5. What does this passage say about God's love and acceptance for us? How are we justified? What produces hope? What is the result of this hope?

1. How do you believe your struggle with comparison connects to your understanding of your identity, value, and acceptance?

2. Can you think of ways you may have used comparison to affirm your normalcy?

3. Can you think of ways you've believed that getting or becoming like an object of your comparison (e.g., another woman's possessions, marriage, or appearance) would help you have a better life?

4. In what ways have you sought approval from others or wondered if you were worthy "enough" of love?

5. What do you think of the statement "shame turns us into shamers?"

Memory Verse: "But God shows his love for us in that while we were still sinners, Christ died for us" (Rom. 5:8).

Lord, make me a Jesus-seeker instead of a better-seeker. Help me to know and feel your love. Teach me to look to you to affirm and define my normalcy, worth, and value. Amen.

Chapter Three

COMPARISON'S CON

*Comparison is the enemy's way of saying,
"God cheated you."*

–Anonymous

He's more scared of me than I am of him.

I chant this in my head but don't believe it. No way that snake's as afraid as I am. And he's coming right at me. *Great. Apparently, I'm not at all intimidating.*

My fight-or-flight response kicks in, and I want to flee before this becomes a crime scene and I'm the victim. But I've nowhere to go. I'm alone in the middle of the swimming pool, lying on a cheap, pink raft that's losing air as quickly as I'm losing courage. I could attempt an Olympic-speed breaststroke to the other side. But I'm a horrible swimmer. It'd look more like a dog paddle. The snake can probably swim twice as fast. Plus, such a move would require me to take my eyes off my opponent. *Never take your eyes off your opponent.*

Panic time. He slithers off the deck into the water. Instinctively, I pull my hands and feet tightly to my body, only to quickly spread them back out again. (Apparently, even weight distribution is the only thing keeping me on this float.) He's less than six feet away now. *I don't want to die this way!* We make eye contact, a truly disturbing experience. How Eve engaged in a whole conversation with one of these creatures—especially before it was condemned to sliding on the ground—is beyond me. Those beady little eyes freak me out. I can't imagine a snake standing beside me and talking. That's what nightmares are made of. I wonder if he can smell my fear? *Do snakes even have noses? Get it together, Heather. It's just a snake.*

I'd visited this pool in my parents' Florida condominium complex dozens of times. How is it that this is the only time I'd ever been completely alone? No witnesses—for either my forthcoming demise or for the really good story that seeing a serpent in the condo pool would make. I glance quickly at the door to the building. I pray Prince Charming will walk through, see me in my peril, dive in, and wrestle the snake to its death. Later, we'll go out to dinner and I'll profusely thank him for *saving my life.*

Alas, no prince.

I hold my breath as the reptile zips right by me to the other side of the pool. He (I'm assuming it's a he—snakes are male and female right? How do you tell that on a snake? I have no idea.) meanders his way to the drain and slithers right up and out onto the pool deck. I watch him disappear into the landscaping. *My life is spared.*

Every time we visit my parents' condo, I recount the story of my brush with death to my children. And, as a shining demonstration of their good sense, they don't go anywhere close to that pool without first checking for snakes. Never mind that he was barely two feet long and green—probably some sort of garden variety. Better safe than sorry, right?

Living the life of comparison is like swimming with a snake in the pool. Yes, there's a chance the hideous creature won't actually bite you. *There's a chance* it will just slither around for a few minutes or an afternoon, maybe even leave you alone. But, let me promise you one thing. As long as there is a snake in the pool with you—you will not be able to relax. You will not feel safe.

From birth, we've learned different patterns of behavior we believe will keep us secure. When faced with danger, we instinctively fight the threat, flee from it, or freeze like a popsicle. Some argue that comparison is a similar instinct. Our brains constantly compare as a way to protect us and preserve our well-being. When we see something unfamiliar, our brain must compare it to what we already know. If it looks like a snake, our brain may classify the danger and determine we should stay away. If it looks like a baby bunny, we likely won't feel threatened.

We do that with each other too, don't we? When we see a woman who physically reminds us of that mean girl in high school, we subconsciously determine to stay away, without any substantive reason, and we may even decide we don't like her. Or we may decide to put too much trust in that guy who resembles our favorite actor. Later, we may find out that our brain's uninformed assessment steered us wrong.

In the early 1950s, Leon Festinger first coined the term "social comparison." He found it a common practice for people to evaluate their opinions and abilities. Some of this, Festinger noted, was good. For example, measuring oneself against an objective standard to know how one is faring (like grades for a college student) can be healthy. But, when no objective measures are available, we tend to use whatever subjective metrics we can find to assess how we're doing.[1] This is when comparison takes the express train to crazy town.

Our brains are hardwired for one thing: survival. Our brains don't want us to grow and learn unnecessarily. They want us to conserve energy, stay in a steady state, and avoid all potential threats. From a young age, we learn what it takes to survive, adapting to what makes our parents happy or keeps our lives most peaceful. As we get older, we continue this adaptation, making subconscious decisions about when it's safe to pursue something and when it's not. Likewise, we subconsciously decide who's safe to befriend, and who's not.

And this is the great danger in living the life of comparison. Our survival-focused craniums convince us that we'll stay safe as long as we *keep* comparing. So we sit on our comfy beds, surrounded by throw pillows, watching other people's lives roll by on Instagram. Scrolling gives us the opportunity to assess ourselves, subjectively, in a hundred different ways. We don't objectively know how we're doing. We only know how we're doing as compared to brief blips from others' online facade.

Intuitively, we understand this. We even participate in it, making determinations on what to share or not share based on how we believe our lives measure up. Date night at the fanciest restaurant in town? *Sure, I'll post that.* Child covered in mud from playing outside? *Yes, that one too. It makes me look like a free-range parent.* Pictures from our staycation at the local Holiday Inn? *No, you don't need to see those. Not when your vacation pictures are from Cancun.* We self-edit our lives based on what sells best on social media. That's not living; that's marketing.

The enemy of our soul knows our propensity toward comparison. With little effort, he can present us with dozens of opportunities to see ways we're "losing" comparison's contest. Combine Satan's tactics with our wired-for-survival brains, and the situation is dangerous. We're becoming a culture of stressed, depressed, and anxious people, who attempt to use the amorphous concept of "enough" as our standard of measure.

Motivation for Change

One day we were traveling home from the West Coast. It was another eight hours of driving before we got to Las Cruces, New Mexico, our stop for the evening. I'm generally pretty picky about where we use the restroom on road trips. But my husband? *Not so much.* I've relaxed a bit—mostly because I carry my own baby wipes and a gallon jug of hand sanitizer—but I do draw the line at using gas station bathrooms with an outside entrance. If I have to go in and get a key attached to some long and disgusting cardboard rectangle, I'd rather hold it. *A girl must have standards.*

Our last stop was designed for truckers. I'd rank the bathroom a six out of ten. Not as nice as Cracker Barrel (no goat's milk hand lotion) but not as bad as the outside entrance bathroom situation. I noticed a sign posted on the back of the stall's door. In red ink, the picture showed a hand throwing a balled-up piece of trash on the floor (where there was already a piece of trash lying). A red slash cut through it: Don't. The picture next to it showed the same hand and ball of trash, only it was painted in green. Here, the hand tosses the ball into the receptacle. Put trash in the can. *Got it.*

Do people really litter out of ignorance? Will this sign really turn the truck stop's litter problems around?

Contrast this with the signs you'll still see all over my state of Texas. They say, "Don't mess with Texas." The campaign started in 1986 to reduce a statewide littering problem. The campaign's goal was to give people a reason not to litter—that is, state pride. And, if you've ever stayed in Texas for more than twenty minutes, you may know that Texans are big on state pride. The campaign motivated people to stop littering.

We need a reason *not* to do things. Most of us know not to compare ourselves to others in the same way that most of us know trash doesn't belong on the floor or along the highway. Yet just knowing the problem exists isn't enough for us to solve it. We need a why—new glasses that allow us to more clearly see how comparison really impacts our lives. I know I'd still be eating bread and brownies if it weren't for my Hashimoto's disease. Even after the doctor's diagnosis, I read books on autoimmune disorders and researched "gluten free," just to make sure she wasn't cheating me out of the joy of baked goods for no reason. Having a clear understanding of the "why" motivates us to change.

The life of comparison may seem safe—familiar. Our parents inadvertently showed us how to do it. Mom complained that the neighbors hired a landscaper and now their yard makes ours "look bad." Dad griped that Bob got the promotion, even though "he's a slacker" and Dad really deserved that raise. Chances are, at some point, Mom or Dad or someone you love measured you against someone else—your sister, your friend, your great aunt Lillabelle who got married before she was old enough to vote. (Okay, maybe that was *just* me. Her name always followed my grandfather's question, "Do you have a boyfriend yet?" *Ugh.*).

And, frankly, not comparing yourself to others? That feels foreign. How can you possibly know how you're doing unless you have someone to compare yourself to? For this reason, Leon Festinger would even tell you that comparison is healthy: "You need it for inspiration." But I disagree. We lose more in comparison than we often realize and need to see the danger before we commit to a way out.

"Thief" Isn't Scary Enough

You've heard the cliché, "Comparison is the thief of joy." But calling comparison a thief understates the ways comparison really hurts us. "Thief" sounds too generic, like a cartoon character wearing a black mask over his eyes or like someone who steals Amazon boxes off people's porches. You're frustrated you've been robbed, but you don't feel like you're in actual danger. The thief wanted your new Kindle. Not you.

"Thief" isn't scary enough unless you remember how much of our comparison is fueled by the enemy of our souls, Satan. Jesus describes this thief's motives in John 10:10: "The thief comes only to steal and kill and destroy. I came that they may have life." Comparison is a thief with many devious talents. He's a swindler who unnerves you with his stealth. *How did he swipe the contentment right out of that moment?* He's a murderer who kills our relationships. And he's a con man who talks us out of peace and then, like an extortionist, drains our joy dry.

The Crime

I'm a plan-through-every-single-detail vacation "prepper." We were headed to Italy for that tenth-anniversary trip, and the one thing I needed more than a guide to gluten-free dining was a pickpocket-proof purse. In Rome, pickpockets are as easy to find as pasta. Thieves target American tourists who are so busy throwing money into the Trevi Fountain and taking selfies that they don't even notice when a sly Italian runs into them and struts away with their wallet.

Like a pickpocket, comparison robs us in subtle ways. We may not actually feel like we've lost anything. But comparison steals from our lives—one handful at a time. Look at this research:

- According to a study released in 2012, people with chronic illnesses who compare their condition to that of others could actually worsen their health issues when they feel they're not doing as well as others battling the same disease.[2]

- Another study examined how comparison and self-criticism impact our ability to accomplish our goals. It found the more you look at others' success and feel "unsuccessful" in comparison, the less likely you are to pursue your dreams.[3]

Comparison not only robs us of our health, but it also stops us from writing that book, taking that trip, applying for that job, or running that marathon.

The Cost of Comparison's Crime

Sometimes comparison doesn't even attempt to steal big things. It just plants a tiny thought and leaves us to feed and water it—until it grows into a full-blown complex! I was in elementary school when I first heard the whisper that my thighs were too large. As I share in my first book, *Compared to Who?*, one little idea started me down a path of comparison, which manifested in my life as disordered eating and fueled body image issues that lasted for decades.

Remember how shame and comparison work together to inspire dastardly ideas in your mind—thoughts that you'd never want anyone to hear? They aren't *really* hurting anyone, are they? Yes, they are. Comparison strikes again. One author makes an interesting observation:

> [W]e found that the happiest people take pleasure in other people's successes and show concern in the face of others' failures. . . . [A] typical unhappy person . . . is deflated rather than delighted about his peers' accomplishments and triumphs and . . . is relieved rather than sympathetic in the face of his peers' failures and undoings.[4]

What you think about other people matters. Comparing yourself to others and feeling behind leads to isolation, depression, eating disorders, anxiety, or worse. Comparing yourself to others and coming out ahead? Let's be honest. No one wants to hang out with the person who obviously feels like she's better than you. So, that takes us right back to loneliness.

Your true adversary is not the object of your comparison, but comparison itself. Here are some more specific ways the crafty criminal of comparison steals from our relationships. These are the ways—both seen and unseen—that comparison actually harms us.

Comparison in Marriage

"The woman who lives across the street from me is ruining my life. She's blonde, tan, and tall like a swimsuit model. She's perfect and she's ruining my life and my marriage. How am I supposed to compete with all that?"

These were the words of a woman I didn't know; she was reaching out for help after reading my blog. We'll call her Renée. Her letter (altered to protect her anonymity) continues:

> How can my husband possibly be happy with me if he keeps seeing her? I'm only 5'3"; I used to be thinner, three children ago.
>
> I'll admit, after our last neighbor moved out, I prayed that anyone but a beautiful young woman would move in. Yet this exact woman became our new neighbor. She's stunning, in fantastic shape. She has a successful career while I've struggled to find a job.
>
> I'm beyond discouraged. Why wouldn't God answer my prayer? I just want to protect my marriage and not have my husband compare me to the young hottie who's

> got it all together. Do you have any advice on how to handle this situation? We can't move at the moment, but this is a strain on our relationship.

Here's a woman literally ready to move (on the stress scale, an event as dramatic as the death of a relative) to get away from comparing herself (or her fear that her husband is comparing). In broad daylight, comparison pilfers Renée's ability to enjoy her marriage. I continued to correspond with Renée, and she shared how her husband feels frustrated when she obsesses. He begs her to understand that he's not comparing her to the woman across the street. But she won't believe him.

Honestly, I used to do the same thing. I'd try to distract my husband when a bikini-clad girl came on TV or when we passed a provocative billboard. I naively thought if I could keep him from ever seeing another beautiful woman, then I'd keep him from comparing me to her. That was the only way I believed I could win. (That or blinding him, which even I recognized was taking it too far.)

Crazy thing, though: he wasn't really comparing me. I was the only one caught in comparison's drama! I fabricated a problem for him and then got mad if he didn't try to solve "his problem" my way. *Call me a generous wife.* As I tried to encourage Renée to see her situation as an internal struggle with comparison—not trouble with her husband or marriage—I sent her this reply:

> I wonder if God allowed this woman to move in to help you overcome your comparison struggles.
>
> The older I get, the more I've come to realize that I'm never going to be the winner of life's beauty contest. There will always be someone thinner, hotter, prettier, more successful. What holds me back in relationships is

> not my lack of a sash and tiara; rather, it's my own damaged perspective.
>
> Even if you move, there will always be another "woman across the street." You can't control it. But, you can control how you view the situation.
>
> Your husband chose you. You've won his heart. Take confidence in the truth that you're his wife. Focus on loving him well and keep your eyes on Jesus, not your "competition."

Another way comparison can affect a marriage relationship is when we compare ourselves *with* our spouses. I used to feel angry and aggravated that my husband would come home tired after work. In my "mother-of-four-under-four" mind, he enjoyed a day with adults, an hour lunch break, and time at the gym afterward. *Poor him.* He had to sit at a desk all day, reading. While I, on the other hand, changed eighteen diapers; potty trained; made breakfasts, lunches, and snacks; wrote the grocery list; and picked up toys for the thirtieth time.

Friend, this kind of comparison creates resentment in your marriage. It robs you of intimacy and stunts your growth as a couple. Relationships have seasons. Some seasons will be harder than others for you; some will be harder on your spouse. Harboring the feelings comparison conjures will do more harm than you know.

Comparison in Friendship

It's not just romantic relationships that comparison destroys. How many of your friendships have been impacted by comparison?

I left my small Christian high school at the end of my junior year and headed straight to college by way of an accelerated admissions program. A group of girls I once counted as confidants resented me for it. They spread rumors. They shut me out. The next June, as the rest of my class entered in pairs of two, I walked alone through that gym to receive my diploma. Michael W. Smith's hit song, "Friends Are Friends Forever" played over the loudspeaker. Ironically, it was our class song.

Realistically, friends may *not* be friends forever. We grow. We change. We move to a new city. But no friendship can stay healthy when comparison creeps in. "Frenemies" pretend to be on your side while, truthfully, they see you as a rival. Friendships that go sideways often start out okay, but then comparison's hug tightens into a chokehold. A friend suddenly seems *too* interested in your life, like she's filling in a mental scorecard. Or, the opposite, a friend may shut you out when something good happens—you get engaged, get pregnant, or get that promotion you wanted. You're left wondering: What happened? I thought we were friends!

Identifying comparison in friendship can be tricky because it's impossible to assess another's motives. The best thing you can do to keep your friendships comparison-free is to pay careful attention to your own thoughts and feelings. For example, when you're planning to meet your friend, are you consumed with what she'll think of you (what you're wearing, the latest stories you have to share), or are you focused on how *she* is doing? When you leave interactions with your friend, do you have to process and (re-process) what kind of impression you made? Or, do you feel like you were able to mutually encourage each other?

Love is the only antidote for comparison inside of our friendships. There's no other magic formula to keeping friendships pure. The only question we can ask ourselves is: Am I loving well? Then, to a lesser extent, we can evaluate whether or not a friend loves us well in return. One caution, though. There's a danger we'll overcomplicate that last part with our own expectations. It's safest to use questions like these as your guide. Is spending time with this friend edifying? Does my friend spur me to be more like culture or more like Jesus?

In 1 Corinthians 13:4, the famous love chapter, the Bible tells us that the existence of envy negates love. "Love is patient and kind; *love does not envy* or boast; it is not arrogant" (emphasis mine). Where there's envy, there's a lack of love. Period. Comparison chokes the life out of all of our relationships. You can't truly love a friend while secretly hating her for being skinnier than you. Neither can you trust a friend who constantly makes comments about you or your life as though she's giving you a grade.

Keeping comparison out of friendship requires frequent heart checks. But, don't let comparison con you into believing that you're better off without friends. No matter how many "mean girls" you've encountered, know that God's desire is for us to engage in meaningful friendships. In fact, bonding with other women heart-to-heart is actually a good way to hamper comparison. Studies show participation in community leads to less comparison.[5] God knew it'd be healthiest to do life with others!

Comparison Demands Discontentment

Another bridesmaid dress. Another wedding in which I'd play a supporting role—when all I wanted was the lead. How many more bouquets did I need to catch to make it my turn? What was I doing wrong? Was I emitting an "I prefer to be single" code detected only by eligible men?

Short of having a husband (a.k.a. the gateway by which all of my dreams would come true), the only thing that could bring me bouts of joy was vacation (or the thought of vacation!). So, participating in a destination wedding had some redeeming qualities. But it felt unfair. She was getting married. I remained single. *Why not me, God? Will I ever get a turn?* Depression with a side of bitterness filled my plate at her reception. I wasn't a very good bridesmaid, not to mention how discontentment prevented me from savoring a great vacation.

Maybe you've landed in the same spot. Comparison deflates dreams and demands discontent. And, if you're already feeling depressed, comparison has an incredibly effective way of making sure you stay that way. Enter social media.

A few years ago, a study looked at how depressed people responded after spending time viewing specially set up Facebook profiles. No shocker here. The more time the depressed person spent looking at the profiles of attractive people, the more envious and depressed he or she grew.[6] Previous studies found similar results. When we believe that our "friends" are living happy, flawless lives—lives that are better than ours—we feel blue. Social media use seems to lead to a now common anxiety condition called FOMO (fear of missing out). Not only do we have more opportunities to compare our lives with the lives of other people than any other generation in history; we're addicted to doing it.

Our grandparents probably knew a few dozen other families. Our parents' circles may have been a little bigger. But in both cases, neither had anywhere near the opportunities to compare themselves to others as we do today. Though most of us haven't actually been inside the homes of most of the people we know, we can (almost) know what their kitchens and bedrooms look like. We know how they decorated their children's rooms, what they made for dinner. We know what they wore on their night out. And we know exactly how many pounds they lost doing Beachbody. All thanks to social media.

Even if you refrain from social networks, there are round-the-clock opportunities to reconcile your ugly to their unbelievable. HGTV shows us a vision of perfect homes with impeccable furnishings, awesome accessories, and to-die-for landscapes. Style networks show us what we should be wearing and what we *should* look like in our clothes. Food Network shows what we should be eating, while DIY Network shows what we could be fixing.

No cable? No problem. You can compare yourself to billboards, magazine covers, or women you see at the community pool. We have a plethora of reasons to compare and unlimited opportunities to allow contentment to disappear, draining our joy faster than the budget on a home improvement show. Life always seems unfair when we compare. Doesn't it?

In church, we hear the words of Paul: "I have learned how to be content with whatever I have" (Phil. 4:11 NLT). The pastor tells us that Paul wrote this from prison, probably after he was flogged. We feel a twinge of guilt. *Even my worst day was better than that.* But how do we flip the switch? "Just be content" doesn't cut it. How do you trade the con of comparison for contentment?

As we continue our journey toward a comparison-free life, I encourage you to stop here and explore how the life of comparison has held you hostage. See clearly where you've been, so you can make your exit. If you've been hunkered down in a life of comparison, now is the time to open the windows, swing wide the doors, and unlock your life. Freedom awaits.

Takeaway

We have to be motivated to want to change our comparison habit. Some of the most compelling "me" reasons to stop comparing include the way comparison harms our relationships (both marriages and friendships), drains our joy, and robs us of contentment.

Comparison-Free Life Action Plan

Read John 10:10, 1 Corinthians 13, John 13:34, and Philippians 4:11, some which are referenced in this chapter.

1. What concepts from these passages can inform our struggle with comparison?

2. Do you agree that comparison is dangerous? If so, in what ways have you seen it cause damage?

3. Think about a time when comparison negatively impacted your ability to feel contentment or experience joy. Did you miss out on the moments of fun or celebration because of comparison's lies? Share this answer with your group or write it down.

4. How has comparison impacted your relationships? Has comparison ever played a negative role in your friendships or marriage (if applicable)?

5. Does social media have an impact on the ways you compare yourself to others in your adult life? Have you ever experienced FOMO (fear of missing out)?

6. Are you motivated to change your comparison habit? Which of the reasons discussed so far in this book have you found most compelling?

7. Spend some time writing in a journal about the ways comparison has kept you trapped. How has comparison stopped you from pursuing your goals? In what ways has comparison inspired a defeatist attitude, depression, or anxiety? Don't just think about these things; write them down so you have a reference point to see how far you've come at the end of this journey.

Memory Verse: "For am I now seeking the approval of man, or of God? Or am I trying to please man? If I were still trying to please man, I would not be a servant of Christ" (Gal. 1:10).

Heavenly Father, please help me recognize how much comparison robs from my life and let go of the things that keep me in its traps. Please bless my relationships and help me give up my comparison habit.

Jill's Story

Food Addiction and the Comparison Trap

A deep depression and bulimia consumed me in college. But years of intense counseling helped me break free of binging and purging. I quit the actions, but not the mind-set of constantly comparing myself to others. "If I were a size two, then I would be happy," I wished. Hating myself was on my mind all the time! I tried many diets only to feel like more of a failure, unable to understand why I couldn't "just be like her."

Eventually, I married, started a family, and had three beautiful boys. But after fifteen years, my marriage hit rock bottom, and I had no support, except from our marriage counselor. Again I went into a deep depression. I knew binging and purging was bad for my body, so I didn't purge. I just binged. My heart was in agony. I struggled, searching for answers on how to recover. The pain was so deep, I can't even accurately describe the darkness that was in me. I found an online BED recovery program and went on my way to recovery. That was the start of truly accepting my body and seeing my identity in Christ.

During my struggle, I clung to Isaiah 61:1–3 as God's promise to me that he was going to give me freedom and turn my ashes into beauty. He promised to turn my spirit of despair into a garment of praise and call me righteous! I couldn't imagine how he could do that, but I continued to pray that verse. I also prayed to know Christ's love for me—to know deep in my soul that he was enough and that he would truly satisfy.

It's been years of Christ meeting me in my mess. I still fight the temptations of food addiction and comparison. I still struggle not to compare myself others, even though I know I am healthy and beautiful. Yet I wouldn't trade my journey for anything, because it's in my deepest darkest nights when I cried out to Jesus that I found him, and I am so in love with Christ!

Chapter Four

ESCAPING THE TRAP

For pride is spiritual cancer:
it eats up the very possibility of love,
or contentment, or even common sense.

–C. S. Lewis, *Mere Christianity*

British royalty fascinates me, and that's why Netflix's show *The Crown* hooked me from the start. Though I've seen other movies and documentaries on Queen Elizabeth, *The Crown* digs into her struggles as England's sovereign, as a wife, and as a woman.

In season two, there's an episode you should definitely skip (trust me) nestled between two you should watch. The first must-see episode is when Queen Elizabeth encounters Billy Graham and wrestles with forgiveness. The second, titled "Dear Mrs. Kennedy," tells a fascinating comparison story—the tale of the queen meeting First Lady Jacqueline Kennedy. Though the queen and Mrs. Kennedy are close in age, Elizabeth watches Jackie on television and complains that she feels old. She anticipates feeling matronly next to the dazzling Jackie, so she worries over finding the right dress for their dinner together. Her stylist says, "When one chooses a gown, one must decide how she wants to feel." Elizabeth replies in subtle confession, "One doesn't want to feel second best. . . ."

On the night of the dinner, while all the men in Buckingham Palace (Elizabeth's husband included) swoon over Jackie, Elizabeth pushes past her self-doubt and attempts to make a friend. Jackie and Elizabeth commiserate over public life, and it seems—for the moment—comparison has been cured through mutual understanding. But gossip separates even the closest of friends, so it doesn't take but a few whispers for insecurity to well up in Elizabeth again. After their meeting, Jackie quips that she found the queen boring, her palace stuffy and outdated. Comparison and self-doubt plague Elizabeth as the harsh words pierce her spirit.

Though the show's writers don't swear to historical accuracy, Internet articles hint there may be some truth to the story. My thought: If even the Queen of England can find someone to compare herself to and fall straight into comparison's trap, it's no wonder you and I take the bait!

Trapped

Do you know how to trap a monkey? According to an old philosophical novel, it doesn't require anything elaborate. All you need is to put some rice inside a coconut with a small opening. The monkey maneuvers his hand inside and grabs the rice. Once his fist clenches tightly around that rice, he can't pull it out of the trap. If he would unclench his fist, he'd easily pull his hand out. But you can count on the monkey to never loosen his grip. He trades a few grains of rice for his freedom.[1]

What if our comparison struggles are really just about our fists being wrapped too tightly around the things we believe we want, need, or deserve for our happiness? Do we stay stuck in comparison's trap, hoping that the next "thing"—be it the man, the promotion, the weight loss, the new house—will set us free when, really, all we need to do to find liberation is loosen our grip?

I don't know what your comparison trap looks like, but I can describe mine. Let's start with the body: mine was never good enough. My large thighs support my bigger-than-I-prefer backside. My calves are strong but too thick to fit into cute riding boots unless they are labeled "extra wide." My nose is too short, as are my fingers. Don't even get me started on my hair. I hated it when it was straight (most of my life), so I curled it daily. After the birth of baby number four, it decided to be curly. Now, of course, I straighten it. In the arena of physical appearance, finding people to compare yourself to is as easy as opening your eyes. The trap taunts me: "Cling to beauty. Find more. Don't let go." My fist clenches around whatever remnant of beauty I can grip. I stay trapped.

But there's more. As a wife, I fall short daily, at least according to what I see in Hallmark Channel relationships. I'm romantically awkward, not at all flirtatious. I don't iron, which probably entitles my husband to file some sort of formal grievance in certain civilizations. My housekeeping skills are less than stellar, mostly because I hate to clean. While we were dating, I spent a full day cleaning before he came over. Turns out he assumed I was a neat freak. (I'm glad he didn't divorce me for false advertising.)

And then there's my mothering. *Ugh.* In my head, I feel like I know how the perfect mom should be. I wake up dreaming and scheming about how to be that woman. She's fantastic. Like Caillou's mom, she never raises her voice, even if the children empty their water guns all over the hardwood floors. This awesome mom in my head, she makes her own chicken nuggets. I've watched the Pioneer Woman do it on her cooking show—but somehow that hasn't magically imparted to me the ability or inclination. They sell frozen dinosaur-shaped ones at Costco, so I buy them. My children deserve homemade chicken nuggets, but I let them down. I can't let go of the list of ways they deserve better.

I'm a homeschool mom, adding another layer to the ways my mothering can fall short. Not only will my children need therapy for their lack of homemade nuggets, but they also run the serious risk of getting to college and forgetting to put their name at the top of the paper. Around the dining room table, page-top monikers are superfluous. But what if not enforcing this habit sets them up for a lifetime of failure? *Sigh.*

The comparison trap teaches me to keep score. To track all wins and losses in my marriage and parenting to make sure I'm staying up to par. But after fifteen minutes on Facebook, I know I'm losing. "Do better!" chants in my head like a fight song.

I hesitate to tell you about the comparison prison that binds me as an author. I almost didn't write this book because I spent so much time reading other books on comparison and comparing myself (and my writing) to them and theirs. *How's that for irony?*

And then there's my walk of faith. I look around church and assume every other woman has fewer struggles than I do. I see *her* on stage and wonder how she keeps her life so together. I find myself longing for a deeper relationship with God, but comparison whispers that I'll never be as "good a Christian" as *she* is.

The life of comparison is one stuck on a treadmill. The control panel tells me I'm going somewhere. I may have walked for miles, uphill even. But if I choose to assess my progress by looking around, it seems I'm stuck in the same place.

The Way of Escape

How do we get off comparison's never-ending treadmill? How do we escape the monkey trap? We have to unclench our fists from what we want for our lives—our ideals, our expectations, and our desires. It's not easy, but freedom is worth it. The Bible tells us that

Satan is the accuser and that he roams the earth looking for whom he can devour (1 Pet. 5:8). Devour? Remember how calling comparison a thief doesn't sound severe enough? What about thinking of comparison as a lion ready to pounce?

First, let's recognize that the enemy wants us to keep comparing. There's no doubt about that. When you compare your life to others' you lack joy, enthusiasm, and motivation to do anything for Jesus. But even more so, the enemy wants us to keep comparing because comparison is sin. *Ouch, right?* It'd be so much more fun if I could just write about how glorious you are, how you don't need to compare yourself to anyone else because you *are* awesome, and that you can work hard to make yourself even awesome-r. (I know, that's not a real word.) But it wouldn't help set you free. I'm not being a good friend to you if I don't show you the truth.

All the memes and many of the quotes used to motivate us to stop comparing focus on "me" reasons. Up until this point, so has this book. *Don't compare because it hurts you, it hurts relationships, and you'll suffer for it.* Now, instead of relying only on the "me" reasons to end comparison, let's turn our attention to the "He" reasons, starting with this truth. Comparison is sin Jesus had to pay for. It hurts the heart of God when we compare.

In a way, the fact that comparison is sin may be the best news you'll hear today. If we can stop writing off our "issues" as merely "things humans struggle with" and instead start calling them out as sin when appropriate, we have great hope of being free from *all* that entangles us.

In my first book, I explained this as it relates to body image. Many women believe body image issues are just "normal girl" problems—that every woman, because she was born female, must struggle with how she looks for her entire life. But when I recognized that the root of my body image issues was actually sin—a problem with beauty and body image idolatry—I found tremendous freedom. Though there's no cure for "normal girl" problems, there is a cure for sin. 1 John 1:9 encourages us with this truth: "If we confess our sins, he is faithful and just to forgive us our sins and to cleanse us from all unrighteousness."

When transgressions are exposed, we have the opportunity to repent and receive forgiveness. Sin separates us from God and will always make our lives feel darker, heavier, and burdened. I wonder if that's why so many of us feel anxious, depressed, and unmotivated after a few minutes of scrolling online. It's tricky. So sneaky, we miss it. But if we want to live comparison-free, we can't ignore the hidden sin lurking under what we categorize as comparison. Sure, it sounds much nicer to say, "I struggle with comparison" than "I struggle with envy." But it's hard to get well unless you accurately diagnose your illness. Our freedom in Christ mandates that we deal with the sin.

Defining the Terms

Part of the reason we don't use terms like jealousy, envy, and covetousness to describe our comparison battles is that we don't confidently know the difference between them.

Let's start with *covetousness*. That's the word we see way back in Exodus when Moses received the Ten Commandments. Exodus 20:17 lays out the command to not covet the following: your neighbor's house, your neighbor's wife, your neighbor's servant, your neighbor's farm animals, or anything that belongs to your neighbor. This seems like a pretty comprehensive list. Coveting is wanting what someone else has, the things they possess. God knew it would be a problem for us, so he put it right there in the Ten Commandments. It's clearly a sin to want your neighbor's new Lexus or Louis Vuitton.

Coveting is hard to detect because the only one who *really* knows you're doing it is you! For this reason, covetousness is a sin against oneself. When we covet, we carry a false belief that getting what we want will satisfy. But it never works out that way. Like greed, covetousness deceives us into always wanting "just a little bit" more. (*Greatest Showman* fans can start singing "Never Enough.") In Luke 12:15, Jesus warns us to guard our hearts against covetousness: "Take care, and be on your guard against all covetousness, for one's life does not consist in the abundance of his possessions."

Envy is more nuanced. Technically envy is defined as what happens when we "lack a desired attribute enjoyed by another."[2] But the word itself derives from the Latin word *invidere*, which literally means to look at someone with a bad attitude. Have you heard the term "the evil eye?" That derived from this same Latin word. Envy happens when she has what you want and you kind of hate her for it.

Simply put, we envy when we want someone else's life. You *can* covet without envying. I'm able to covet my neighbor's newly remodeled kitchen, comparing her granite countertops to my peeling laminate, without hating her for it. But envy adds an extra layer of having negative feelings toward the person who has what I want. If I privately refer to my neighbor as "Miss Perfect House" or avoid inviting her over because I fear her opinion of my counters, I reveal a spirit of envy. My words tattle on the envy happening in my heart.

If your comparison struggle includes wrestling body image, know that both covetousness and envy can be at play. Sometimes we envy a beautiful woman, desiring to have the same level of beauty she does—perhaps feeling aggravated or annoyed that *she's* so gorgeous. Other times, we check out the woman on the cover of the magazine and objectify her. Not seeing her as human, we long to have the same sculpted arms or thin thighs, subconsciously classifying them as possessions instead of body parts. We don't care so much about her; we just covet her assets.

Psychologists suggest that there are two types of envy. Malicious envy wants someone to be ruined or "leveled down" because of what she has, while benign envy is a positive motivational force that aspires to "level up" to having as much as or being as good as the object of envy.[3] Though psychologists say benign envy is healthy, the apostle Paul calls all envy sin—evidence of walking in the flesh instead of the Spirit (Gal. 5). Envy flows from the heart, defiling a person. Proverbs 14:30 tells us, "A tranquil heart gives life to the flesh, but envy makes the bones rot." Envy can negatively impact everything, including our health.

Then there's *jealousy*. While envy is motivated by feelings of inferiority, jealousy is motivated by feelings of loss. It occurs when something we already have feels threatened.[4] If a woman is flirting with your husband, you feel jealous. If a friend gets the promotion that you applied for, you experience jealousy. Jealousy can be suspicious (i.e., your husband's office just hired a cute new admin and you fear your husband may notice). Or it can be reactive and founded in truth (i.e., your husband really *is* spending too much time with the new admin and it concerns you). When you're jealous, you feel sad or lonely, frustrated that you may lose something you love.

Though God can be jealous without tainting his holy character, envy is always a sin. According to Galatians 5:19–21, we need to beware of both:

> Now the works of the flesh are evident: sexual immorality, impurity, sensuality, idolatry, sorcery, enmity, strife, jealousy, fits of anger, rivalries, dissensions, divisions, envy, drunkenness, orgies, and things like these. I warn

> you, as I warned you before, that those who do such things will not inherit the kingdom of God.

I don't know about you, but I don't think I would have included my struggles with comparison on a list this extreme. *Orgies? Sorcery? Sexual immorality?* Certainly my struggle with desiring her firm abs, her cushy job, or her incredible vacation home couldn't be as bad as those other things on the list! As a teen, several of my friends received purity rings to remind them to save sex for marriage. But I don't think I've ever seen a piece of jewelry that reminds young girls not to envy. *Hmmm* . . . yet God has got them right here on the same list, as if they're equally wrong.

One day, my daughter came home from church proudly displaying a paper cup decorated with an upside-down "Love does not envy" sticker. I assumed it was some sort of system to discourage comparison—like a "swear jar" where you put in a quarter every time you envy. Alas, she said it was just a way to display the verse. (Which is why the sticker was on the wrong way. I'm glad to know she was following directions.) But it got me thinking: if envy is as bad as the Bible says it is, perhaps we should all have "envy jars."

Sure, every sin has unique consequences. Yet I've heard various ministers explain the ways that covetousness, jealousy, and envy are gateway sins. Look back at that list from Galatians 5. I've personally seen jealousy and envy lead to rivalries, dissensions, and divisions. Ever been angry when a friend got something you wanted? It seems "fits of anger" can be inspired by comparison's secret sins as well. Classic television murder mysteries always featured a killer motivated by jealousy, while coveting usually precedes stealing and adultery. Now, I'm not saying that because you struggle with comparison you're going to turn into a criminal. But it's worth mentioning again that these sins hidden in our "comparison" vernacular aren't as innocent as we may assume.

And then there's *pride*. Pride is such a confused term in our culture, isn't it? I hear Christian women talk about "taking pride" in their gardens or children, and it almost fools me into believing that pride is healthy. At the same time, I hear about groups marching over pride in things that are contrary to the Bible, and it somehow feels clear that pride is sin.

Google defines pride as "a feeling or deep pleasure or satisfaction derived from one's own achievements." I can be proud of the cake I made. (Okay, because I'm such a bad baker, I'll likely never be proud of a cake I made, but you get my point.) That doesn't seem sinful. But, in the realm of comparison, pride always begs the answer to this question: "How am I doing *as compared* to you?" If I'm doing well, I "take pride" in the way I'm winning this (completely fabricated) contest. If I'm faring worse, pride allows me to wallow in despair. The low side of pride says, "I'll never be enough. No matter what I do." Do you see the shadow of envy in each of these responses?

Pride isn't just thinking too highly of you; it also works in reverse. Thinking too lowly of you feeds self-absorption. Keeping score, grading everyone you see, and then evaluating yourself constantly isn't just an unhealthy exercise—it's a sinful one. You may have heard that the reason we get stuck in comparison is low self-esteem. *If only we could feel more confident in our bodies and our abilities, then we'd have no reason to compare.* But self-focus is a trap that requires us to compare ourselves even more. There's no objective standard of measure—so we have to keep comparing in order to muster a shallow confidence. High self-esteem and low self-esteem are two sides of the pride coin. Comparison isn't a result of low self-esteem; it's a shallow understanding of grace.

Like any other sin, pride can lead us to dangerous places. The Bible is clear on how God feels about pride: "God opposes the proud but gives grace to the humble" quickly comes to mind and is found twice in Scripture (James 4:6 and 1 Pet. 5:5). I love how C. S. Lewis clearly describes pride in *Mere Christianity*: "Unchastity, anger, greed, drunkenness, and all that, are mere flea bites in comparison: it was through Pride that the devil became the devil: Pride leads to every other vice: it is the complete anti-God state of mind."

Want to get rid of this type of pride? C. S. Lewis has a suggestion: "Pride gets no pleasure out of having something, only out of having more of it than the next man. . . . *It is the comparison that makes you proud*: the pleasure of being above the rest. Once the element of competition is gone, pride is gone" (emphasis mine).[5] Cutting out comparison allows us to live a life of humility and gives us the ability to receive God's grace.

If you're feeling a little down after reading this chapter, please don't. I want to encourage you. No matter how deep into the pit of comparison you've fallen, there's always a way out. You haven't out-sinned God's ability to save you. The Bible tells us that we've *all* fallen short; we've all sinned (Rom. 3:23). Maybe today is the first day you ever felt the weight of that sin. Or maybe today is the first day you see how comparing yourself to other people may actually be a sinful practice. No matter where you're at—embrace grace. Don't wallow where you've been. Rather, confess, repent, and ask God to help you live differently from this day forward.

This Life Is Not the Main Event

At age twenty-four, I took a trip abroad for a graduate school class. I'll just call it what it was—a vacation for which I earned four graduate school credit hours. It's an unbeatable deal, really. Except for the fact that I needed a student loan to pay for it. (My husband is still a little upset about paying for that trip a decade later, after we got married, so don't bring it up around him, okay?)

The itinerary consisted of travel to Israel and England. I felt like the worst Christian ever for thinking this, so I never said it out loud, but I didn't *really* want to go to Israel. It scared me—the Middle East isn't the safest place to visit. And safety is a big issue to me (reference my number seven Enneagram score). But I dreamed of London. Big Ben. Westminster Abbey. Buckingham Palace. St. Paul's Cathedral (where Princess Di got married). I wanted to go there. Ride the Tube. Eat some bad pub food and buy a teacup at Harrods.

One of the most curious things listed on our London itinerary was attending the Queen's Birthday Parade. *How fabulous would that be?* I assumed the powers that be timed this trip perfectly so we could witness something that amazing. Not only was I going to England, I was actually going to see the queen! *Could life get any better?*

Months later, after weeks of travel, the big event arrived. We ate the American breakfast in our dank and dingy hotel. We headed to the appointed parade-watching spot. It seemed odd that more Londoners weren't staking out a place on the sidewalk with lawn chairs and blankets. In my hometown in Pennsylvania, people start claiming their spots along the road a full day before the Fourth of July parade. Wouldn't the Queen's Birthday Parade bring out the crowds? Maybe Brits weren't into this sort of thing?

When our tour guide Steve finally arrived, he clarified that we weren't there to see the actual parade—just the dress rehearsal for the parade. The queen's staff would walk through the parade route as practice for the event slated for next week. Minutes later, one carriage passed by holding a member of the London Police Department. *Wow!* That was underwhelming. *Are you kidding me?* I could write an entire book on all the foibles from this trip thanks to this "special" guide, but for the sake of this illustration, I'll leave it at this. When you think you're going to watch the queen on parade and instead see one not-even-close-to-famous guy in a carriage, it's quite a letdown.

Friends, we too often believe this life is *the* parade. But it's just the dress rehearsal. Nothing on this earth can satisfy us in the ways that we crave. Even the greatest thrills here (and there are thrills—from wedding days to babies' birthdays to unforgettable vacations and earthly dreams coming true) are a lame substitute for what is to come. There's going to be no comparison. Seeing our lives as the main event—where we're the star, writing our own destiny—cultivates a culture of comparison. Our hearts can't rest when our lives depend on our ability to keep up. There's no set point where we can ever find "enough." We have to keep looking to other people to see how we're doing, where we rank. We can be billionaires and still compare watches. We can literally be the Queen of England and still wrestle comparison's quandary.

Comparison is a disease of the heart. Even the best "me" reasons to cure comparison fail until we understand the "He" reasons. We could get everything we desire and find that towers of gold are still too little. Pride is never satisfied and envy fears rest. Only the grace of Jesus and a heart of gratitude will lead us to joy, peace, and rest.

Takeaway

Comparison is our culture's catchall term for things God calls sin—namely, covetousness, envy, pride, and sometimes jealousy. For us to be free from comparison's grip, we must recognize how these sins harm us and separate us from the heart of God. Until we deal with the sin in our hearts regarding comparison, we can't find freedom.

Comparison-Free Life Action Plan

Read the following Scriptures referenced in this chapter: Exodus 20:17, Luke 12:15, Proverbs 14:30, Romans 12:3, Galatians 5, Philippians 2:3, James 4:6, and 1 Peter 5:5. What do you observe from these passages about covetousness, envy, jealousy, and pride?

1. Are you comfortable calling comparison's roots—pride, covetousness, and envy—sin? Does this feel difficult for you?

2. Are you clear on the differences between covetousness, envy, and jealousy? Do you think it's important to understand the distinctions?

3. In what ways do you think we can keep ourselves from the prevalent sin and help our sisters in Christ who battle it daily?

4. If (plausibly) even the Queen of England struggles with comparison, what does that tell you about winning its game? Is there ever a status or destination we can reach where we'd be free from comparison outside of embracing Jesus's grace and walking in the Spirit?

5. Take a few minutes to confess, in your journal or out loud, the hidden sin in your personal struggles with comparison. Confess as specifically as you can the ways you've envied, coveted, or relied on pride to feel like you measure up. If you're

comfortable, share these with your group or with a friend. Then repent, seek, and embrace God's forgiveness together.

Memory Verse: "For by the grace given to me I say to everyone among you not to think of himself more highly than he ought to think, but to think with sober judgment, each according to the measure of faith that God has assigned" (Rom. 12:3).

Heavenly Father, I acknowledge today the ways that I've sinned against you in the area of comparison. Forgive me for my covetousness, my envy, and my pride. Help me to recognize these sins when they tempt me. Thank you for your forgiveness and teach me how to walk a new path.

Chapter Five

THE IDEAL ME

Inside every cynical person, there is a disappointed idealist.

–George Carlin

From the other room, I hear my children open and close the fridge door and shuffle through cardboard boxes in the pantry. They're hungry. *Again.* (It's been like an entire half hour since they ate.) As they grab for another granola bar, I add a checkmark to my Mom Fail list.

Remember that perfect mom I long to be? There's more to her than homemade chicken nuggets. She always has healthy snacks at the ready. She gets home from Costco, cleans and cuts eighty pounds of vegetables, then places them into glass storage containers (no BPA here, folks). Some days, she treats her offspring to baked goods—fashioned from combinations of organic oats, raw honey, and fruits she dehydrated herself.

When she's not in the kitchen, she crafts with her children (who are dressed like Gap models). Instead of throwing away their

Sunday school papers, she finishes the incomplete parts with them around the dining room table. She maintains a good mood. You know why, of course. It's because she gets up three hours before her children to run five miles, spend an hour in devotions, clean the house, and prepare their gourmet breakfast so that the scent of sizzling bacon stirs those children from their slumber. She is the Proverbs 31 woman.

But I'm just an average mom. I buy that same ten-pound bag of carrots and jam it into the fridge drawer, only to use it when a recipe forces my hand. While those potential snacks rot away in a drawer no one can open, my children feast on tortilla chips and granola bars. *Lots of granola bars.* I have other mom fails too. I meant to teach them each a second language by age five. (You know, during those years when they'd retain it best.) I also planned to have "outdoor exercise time" daily. Instead, we watched the Spanish videos once before I gave up and sold them. We walked to the park last week, and I may get up the energy to do that again. *Someday.*

I'm sometimes tempted to skip the last chapter in Proverbs when it comes up in my Bible reading plan, just because it reminds me of how far I am from the ideal mom I wanted to be. This mom in my head is so fantastic, I can't compete. Comparing myself to her is a beatdown. But that's different than comparing myself to other people, isn't it?

Compared to Me?

I meet many women who share with me this one simple sentiment: I don't compare myself to others, I just compare myself to the self *I* want to be. (That's a mouthful.)

What they're saying is that it's not that they feel like they can't keep up with Sara down the street. Rather, it's that they can't keep up with the person—be it the mom, wife, or woman—they wish they could be. They say things like, "I can't live up to my own standards." Or, "I don't feel like a failure because of not looking like *her* or doing things like *her*. . . . I feel bad because I don't measure up to what and who *I* wanted to be." Or even, "I just want to be more like I *used* to be."

It's called idealization. Sometimes when we idealize someone else it can more aptly be classified as objectification. These are the situations where we idealize and project other positive attributes onto a person just because she has a hot body or fabulous career. But other times we just park our trailer in the land of self-idealization. Our engines stall and we never leave, because it's too heavy a weight for us to haul. When a woman tells me, "I don't compare myself to celebrities . . . or other people . . . just to the me I want to be," my first question is always, Where did this "ideal self" come from?

Years ago, when I talked to a counselor about my body image struggles, he encouraged me to find a picture of my ideal self. It was the craziest assignment. I didn't even know where to start. But as I combed through hundreds of images of different women, I realized that my ideal self looked a whole lot like a Miss America contestant circa 1985. Growing up, I watched the pageant every year, so I knew her type well. Her hair was fluffy. Her legs were thin. And she looked great playing the violin in a ball gown. Even the official Miss America Pageant song reinforced my belief: "There she is, Miss America. There she is, your ideal."

This exercise stunned me. Subconsciously, I felt internal pressure to look like a twenty-something beauty queen from the 1980s. Ridiculous, right? But in my heart, I knew it was true. I longed to look like that and be someone's ideal. Though there are thousands of unique ways to be physically beautiful, there was one particular type of beauty in my head that I felt I should try to match. I didn't feel pressure to be beautiful like Taylor Swift, Kim Kardashian, or even Heidi Klum. A specific ideal of beauty was driving me.

If you're motivated by a certain beauty ideal, parenting ideal, marriage ideal, you name it—stop and ask yourself where these ideals originated. When pressed, most of us would admit that we've fallen victim to culture's marketing ploys. Some of them are direct, like "Get smooth skin" ads or Nutrisystem commercials that imply we all need to lose weight. It's no secret that advertisers purposefully drive us to feel dissatisfied and want more. Some are subtler, like a friend's pictures on social media. You see the perfectly staged photo. A woman is lying by the beach, but you only see her legs. Then you spend fifteen minutes staring at yours, wondering if they'd look skinnier from that angle. (Of course, then you find out it wasn't legs at all—just a picture of two hot dogs by the ocean! Google it. Trust me, you'll laugh.)

If you stop and pray about where your "ideal self" concepts came from, I bet you'll find the same truth I did. They weren't actually *in* me; they were inspired by an outside force and, somewhere along the way, adopted as my own. If it feels like an imaginary force drives your "quest for a better me," I encourage you to peel back the layers of your belief. Chances are, your expectations are influenced more by outside forces than you realize. Comparing our current selves to our "former" selves or "ideal" selves isn't really that different from other types of comparison.

Idealism Is Idolatry

When we idealize, we idolize.

The truth is, that perfect mom I fantasize about isn't just an ideal—she's an idol. Now, don't get me wrong. I don't sacrifice Costco chicken nuggets to her statue on my lawn. (Frankly, we have no nuggets to spare.) Modern-day idolatry doesn't look like Old Testament idolatry. In his book *Counterfeit Gods,* Timothy

Keller explains more about modern-day idols: "An idol is whatever you look at and say, in your heart of hearts, 'If I have that, then I'll feel my life has meaning, then I'll know I have value, then I'll feel significant and secure.'"[1]

That hot-bodied, always calm, natural-food-prepping mom in my head is an idol. She tells me that my life will be better when I become her. She keeps me chasing after her, like a child chasing a squirrel at the park. Though I never catch her, it feels like an attainable goal. Even if I don't do anything obvious to try to be more like my ideal, on the inside I suffer emotionally for not measuring up to her standards of greatness. Her verdict "You're failing! Do better!" zaps my zest for life.

Recognizing this, sometimes women ask me a related question: "Heather, I know it's wrong to strive like this. So, how do I just accept myself? Shouldn't I want to like who I am?"

Answering this tricky question requires us to see how idealization can put us in the dangerous position of idolizing ourselves and our own opinions. God never commands us to try to keep ourselves happy. Though our culture has practically made self-acceptance a threshold for mental health, the Bible says something different. In 1 Corinthians 4:3, Paul shares that he doesn't even judge himself. In other words, his opinion of himself (read: self-acceptance) doesn't matter as much as God's opinion of him. Living to please ourselves, or trying to become our ideal in order to make ourselves happy, serves the god of self, not the God of the universe.

Jesus Doesn't Ask You to Be Like Her, He Asks You to Be Like Him

Maybe your ideal *isn't* a figment of your imagination. Maybe she's someone you know. Perhaps you watch in awe as she finishes spin class without sweating. (As previously established, I have a problem with idolizing women who don't appear to sweat.) Somehow, when she walks through the wind, it blows her hair into an even more attractive style. (I walk in the wind and my hair mats to my lipstick. I find "Touch of Taupe" stained hairs the rest of the day.) Or maybe she's the woman who does it all. She can run the PTA, run marathons, run the soup kitchen, all while keeping her toilets, toddlers, and toenails pristine.

Friend, I'm not going to waste words telling you that you don't know what she's "really" going through. Sure, the better you get to know this woman, the more likely you would be to see she's not as perfect as you assume. But that's not a sufficient answer to your idealization problem. Hopefully this is: Jesus didn't call you to be her. He doesn't ask you to look around and identify the women you admire and try to become like them. At the risk of sounding too extreme, "fitspiration" is demonic. Putting our time, energy, and emotional and financial capital into being like another woman is idolatry, driven by envy, covetousness, or pride. It's not just a "thing" you need to work through; it's something God hates. It's time to stop.

And the same goes for chasing your personal ideal. She's just an idol too. The longer you compare yourself to her, the more you'll stay stuck in discontentment. What's the vision board of your heart look like? Remember, the only person God asks you to become more like is Christ.

Covetousness connects to idolatry because when we covet, we allow our desire for things to take equal footing with our desire for Jesus. Check out Ephesians 5:5: "For you may be sure of this, that everyone who is sexually immoral or impure, or who is covetous (that is, an idolater), has no inheritance in the kingdom of Christ and God." Again, in Colossians 3:5, Paul instructs, "Put to death therefore what is earthly in you: sexual immorality, impurity, passion, evil desire, and covetousness, which is idolatry." Paul sounds serious to me. No inheritance? Put to death? We can't love Jesus *and* covet a little. There's no biblical option for that.

How much of our idealism is rooted in a love for this world or, as the Bible calls it, pride of life? Do we live as if this life is what matters the most? Have our hearts elevated things—even good things— into ultimate things? Have we placed our images, ideals, dreams, or expectations into a position reserved for Jesus alone? Do I want the new furniture because it helps me be hospitable when I have the neighbors over, or do I want to impress them?

Read what John has to say in 1 John 2:15–17:

> Do not love the world or the things in the world. If anyone loves the world, the love of the Father is not in him. For all that is in the world—the desires of the flesh and the desires of the eyes and pride of life—is not from the Father but is from the world. And the world is passing away along with its desires, but whoever does the will of God abides forever.

Later in the same book, John offers this reminder: "Little children, keep yourselves from idols" (1 John 5:21). John, the beloved disciple, is not talking to children; he's writing to Christian adults. But he knows idolatry tempts us like a stranger offering Snickers bars to kids.

What No One Tells You about Your Ideal

During our travels, my daughter Katie and I took a walk down the mountain at a friend's house in Cerro Piñon, New Mexico. She stopped frequently to pick up interesting stones. But one especially caught her eye. "Mom, is this gold?" she asked me.

It did look like gold, especially the way the sun reflected off it. Rocks always fascinated me as a little girl too. My grandfather kept his favorite finds in a glass coffee table, where he displayed his impressive collection of polished stones. I enjoyed collecting them too, and even carried a little identification book to help. So I knew, with certainty, the truth: it wasn't real gold. I consoled her that she wasn't alone in mistaking it for gold. Miners during the gold rush were continually fooled by a rock called pyrite—or fool's gold—because it looks so much like the real thing. All these ideals—idols—we chase. Friends, they're fool's gold too.

I thought having a book published would make me happy.

Others told me it wouldn't. I went to the seminars and heard best-selling authors talk about feeling despair after their sixth *New York Times* best seller failed to sell a million copies. I took notes. And then I did what so many of us do. I believed this little lie in my head: *Well, that's how it worked for him, but I know it'll be different for me. If I had that, I know I'd be content.*

So my first book was published, and I set out to do what they tell you to do as an author selling books in the twenty-first century—get enough people to buy it so you can earn a "#1 best seller" flag in your book's category on Amazon. Once you have it, you can tell people your book was number one. Even if it was only number one in the "books for people with albino dogs" category, you can still honestly tell people you hit the top. I'm type A enough not to let an opportunity for merit pass me by, so I scrambled. I wrote friends from middle school and random strangers whose friend requests I'd accepted—begging them to buy.

Slowly, the book started crawling up the charts. I went to bed at number two. If I were a younger woman, I would've stayed up to finish the job, but I always prioritize sleep. At around three A.M., a child walked into our bedroom, saying, "Mom, my stomach doesn't feel good. I think I'm going to . . ." You can guess what happened next. Fortunately, she made it to the toilet. I put beach towels all over her sheets and gave her a large orange plastic bowl to sleep with. (Yes, my life is glamorous.) As I walked back toward my bedroom, I decided to sneak a peek at my computer. *What's this? I made it to number one!* The book climbed to the top while I slept. I quickly took a screenshot, since I knew it wouldn't last long. The next day, exhausted, I decided a relaxing bath was in order. Want to know what I thought of while in that bathtub? I thought about how I should quit writing. I thought about shutting down my blog, canceling all my speaking engagements, and giving up the whole thing. Reaching my goal didn't make me happy.

God has shown me this truth in other areas of life too. I hit my goal weight decades ago, yet still struggled to feel body confident. Now, as I sit here wearing many extra pounds, the shine of the fool's gold still taunts me in an eerie voice: "If you could get thin again, you'd be happier. Try it. Find a new diet. It'll make you feel good." I thought marriage would make me happy. That dream shattered before we boarded the flight home from our honeymoon.

Children, motherhood . . . they were supposed to satisfy me too. Raising babies drained more than it filled. We built a brand-new house a few years ago. My kitchen beamed with white cabinets and subway tile, while dark wood floors stretched from the front door to the back. It was so pretty. But, can I confess? By the time we moved out, I'd developed a passionate hatred toward those high-maintenance floors and hard-to-keep-clean cabinets.

All these ideals were idols that sparkled like gold. I thought I could load my bag with them and be rich. Instead, I was burdened, carrying around a bag of rocks. We look for joy, peace, and contentment in so many places other than Jesus. Then we're surprised when we can't find it. That's idolatry's game. The good news is: you don't have to play it. Once you see it, you can set a new course. We'll talk about this more in Section Two.

Expectations

Idealism has a close cousin. You may be familiar with her. I call her expectations. And God used a decade's worth of Mother's Days to teach me her ways.

I'd experienced at least a dozen absolutely horrible, no good, very bad Mother's Days before my oldest son even turned five. Mother's Day misery started *well* before I read "pregnant" on a pee-covered stick. I wanted so badly to be a mom. Nothing would make me as happy as having a baby. *Those sweet baby smiles. Those warm baby cuddles. All those cute little outfits.* . . . I idolized the concept of motherhood. So I was annually reminded—in a loud and quite obnoxious way—that I lacked the one thing I *knew* would fulfill me. For years, my biological clock ticked loudly, yet I had no reason to receive any honors on the second Sunday in May.

Then it happened. In February of 2006, I found out I was pregnant. Anxious to start celebrating the holiday I'd been *robbed* of for all those years, I observed my first Mother's Day the next year. Let me tell you how wonderful it was . . . I finally joined the mommy club. Now I could wait in bed for my breakfast and roses to come on a classy tray. I'd enjoy spa treatments and relish the celebration of me—and the magnificent way I ushered new life into this world. Only this didn't happen. *Staying in bed? Hello?* I was breastfeeding a six-month-old. I don't even remember what my husband did (there was likely a gift card involved), but I assure you it was not enough. Whatever he gave, whatever he helped with, I was so focused on me that he didn't have a chance of getting it right.

This trend continued. Skip ahead several years. Did I mention my husband became a pastor? The reality that Mother's Day always falls on a Sunday stung me like an angry bee. My attitude during those first few years of Mother's Day solo parenting was less than joyful. Coincidentally, on those *same* Sundays, members of our young congregation would have brunch plans so they *couldn't possibly* help with the children's classes as scheduled. Yes, I'd get the privilege of caring for *all* of the children in our church that morning too. You know, after feeding and dressing my four, by myself, on Mother's Day! Bitterness oozed out of me like a Hot Pocket left in the microwave too long.

My struggle wasn't limited to Mother's Day. I've spent some miserable Christmases, birthdays, and anniversaries too. I suffer from a disease called chronic disappointment disorder, or CDD. Okay, it's not a real thing, so don't ask your doctor about it. I just made it up. But it affects me (and my appreciation of life in general) in very real ways. Lest I bore you by recounting all of my holiday letdowns, let me tell you a little secret. I finally figured out how to make Mother's Day and every holiday enjoyable. It only took me a decade. I really wish I'd figured it out sooner.

Because of my CDD, I also have a hard time appreciating gifts. The present could be great—really great, even. But if it's not what I hoped for, I feel let down. The other side of this equation is equally challenging. If I tell you what I want, and you get it for me, then I feel disappointed. You only got it because I asked. It's truly a lose-lose. *My poor husband.* I bet you can relate. Expectations get us into trouble all the time, don't they? We get an idea in our head of how things should go, or be, or look, and then when they fall short, we crumple like a used lunch bag.

We're told to believe it's the level of our expectations that causes the actual problem. So we play mind games, trying "not to expect anything." To me, this is akin to saying, "Don't think about pink elephants." As soon as you say something that outrageous, it's all your brain can focus on. Don't expect roses (though flowers are "what I deserve"). Don't expect dinner (though he's a jerk if he thinks I'm going to cook today). Don't expect (fill in your favorite gift here).

It doesn't work. But I have found a better solution. God has worked to heal my CDD and show me that the best way to enjoy my holidays (and every day, no matter the circumstances) is to take the focus off of myself. When I got my mind off of me, I changed. I saw how—particularly in the case of Mother's Day—I'd made motherhood (and the celebration of motherhood) an idol. After repentance and confession, I shifted my focus from ungratefulness for what I "missed out on" and shifted to thankfulness for what God *had* blessed me with. When I stopped thinking about me, I was able to relax. I felt free. And guess what? So did everyone around me.

God taught me this lesson in my marriage, in my ministry, and in my friendships too. Nothing ruins a good relationship faster than unspoken expectations. Isn't that the path our idealism and expectations take us down? We fall in love with our dreams, our desires. We idolize them, worshipping them in place of God. And then, even if they do come true, they disappoint. It's not enough to make us happy. Comparison fuels our expectations. Then, if we look closely, it reveals our idols.

Get Out of My Chair

I'll confess, sometimes I still fantasize about living my ideal life. The older I get, the more this fantasy morphs from dreaming of great beauty to dreaming of wild career success.

Wouldn't it be amazing if I could do what Brené Brown did—give a ten-minute Ted Talk that went viral—and suddenly I'm speaking to audiences of thousands and recording my own Netflix special? There'd be so many opportunities flooding my inbox. More books, arena events, morning talk shows. Sure, it might be a pain getting stopped all the time to do selfies with random strangers. But I'd always be kind and give my followers something "Insta worthy." Stardom wouldn't go to my head. I'm sure.

I'd do it all for Jesus, of course. I'd share his truth and graciously accept any awards by thanking "my Lord and Savior" before mentioning my husband, my mom, and my agent. Humbly, I'd shrug off their praise through my sheepish smile. They'd lead me to my place on stage, and I'd sit in that chair of honor feeling pleased that I was able to bring light and hope to the masses.

Suddenly, Jesus walks in. *He's here because he's so pleased. How could he not be? I'm doing this all for him.* As he comes on stage, some clap. It's a little awkward that he didn't make a better entrance, but I go with it. Perhaps he's coming to give me my heavenly crowns early. I smile at him as he takes those last few steps toward me. Then I hear him say something unexpected.

"Heather, get out of my chair." *Ouch.*

Friend, isn't that just how pride works in our lives? It subtly invites us to honor our expectations and ideals. When we feed on self-esteem snacks instead of the nourishing truth of God's word, we can start to believe that we *should* have more, we *should* be more. Secretly, we believe we deserve our wishes, our wants, and our desires. They're entitled to a throne.

But then Jesus gently reminds us that there isn't room for two in his chair.

Bridging the Grand Canyon

When our family visited the Grand Canyon, my travel-weary preteens were less than thrilled. My daughter's exact words were, "Yeah, it's a giant hole in the ground. How long do we have to spend looking at it?" Granted, there's magnificent beauty in this natural wonder. But my children couldn't see it. They saw what was missing instead of what was there—a spectacularly carved chasm.

Most of us live with an acute awareness of the space between who we are and who we want to be. We know what's missing. We want to be better, but the gap feels unsurpassable. A nagging voice in our heads tells us that happiness awaits on the other side of that great divide, if only we could get there—if only we could bridge the gap. And we believe it. It drives our comparison. It fuels our striving. It may even motivate us to be healthier, work harder, finish school . . . you name it.

The problem is that the landmass on the other side of that canyon—that "better" place we believe we should reach—is very much the same as the land on this side of the canyon. As my children astutely observed, we could take the tour bus around the whole south rim of the Grand Canyon and, though the view may be different, we'd still be looking at the same hole. We'd still be in Arizona, still standing on similar soil.

Some believe they've found a way to bridge the chasm to their ideal self. They've set weight loss or business goals and met them. But, when they cross, they still find themselves standing on a rim. They try to cross again, believing they can do better, be better. Yet they only find a new spot on the crater's border. Again, they're still standing on a rim. Contentment eludes them. This has happened to me more times than I care to confess while on my quest for self-improvement.

So, if we can't bridge the gap by becoming our ideal, what do we do? Will we never be content?

That chasm we all feel, God put that inside us. It's a longing, a desire for something greater. This holy dissatisfaction was designed to draw us to God, to find satisfaction in him alone. Trying to bridge this chasm by becoming more "ideal" never satisfies because the gap we really need to fill isn't between an earthly idea of perfection and ourselves; it's between us and a perfect God. The only way to span that gap is with grace.

This may sound oversimplified to you, especially if—like me—you grew up in church and feel you've heard all the "God and Jesus" answers. But stick with me, friend. Grace's borders extend far beyond our worship song lyrics; its abyss is far deeper than our imaginations can dive. God's magnificent grace is intermingled in every minute of our daily lives. And, once we can see with new eyes the miracle of grace, we'll be able to stop comparing and start living.

Takeaway

Comparison can fuel idealism and idolatry. When we rely on our expectations or ideals to satisfy us, we're never able to rest. Comparison's canyon can only be crossed with God's grace, not through achieving our ideal.

Comparison-Free Life Action Plan

Read these passages, some of which are referenced in this chapter: Ephesians 5:5, Colossians 3:5, 1 John 2:15–17, and 1 John 5:21. What do you learn about idols (remember these are also our "ideals") in these verses?

1. What is it you can't live without? Do you ever have that "I'll die if I can't have this" feeling? Is it a relationship? A new home? A better job? A title or a certain degree?

2. In what scenarios do you become most defensive? Do you tend to feel combative when someone questions your intelligence? Your parenting? Your political views? Look for idols of pride disguised as issue-centric zeal.

3. Fill in this sentence as honestly as you can: I'll be happy when ____________________. This may be the easiest way to spot an idol. It could be that you long for something good, like a baby or a more intimate relationship with your husband. But we can still twist good things into ultimate things. God wants our hearts to be satisfied only in him.

4. Think of a woman you admire. Now check your heart as you ask yourself this question: Is it a bigger compliment for someone to say you look or act like this woman, or that you look or act like Jesus?

5. Journal about the idols Jesus reveals to your heart. This will be a process. We'll talk more about idols in Chapter Eight, where you'll be prompted to make a more extensive list. For now, write a prayer surrendering any idols to him.

Memory Verse: "Those who pay regard to vain idols forsake their hope of steadfast love" (Jon. 2:8).

Heavenly Father, help me to stop idealizing and idolizing other people or my own wants and goals for my life. Help me to stop bowing to the gods of my ideals and expectations and, instead, humbly trust you to meet all my needs. Thank you for your work in my heart. Amen.

Becca's Story

Confessions of a Compare-aholic

My name is Becca, and I'm a chronic compare-aholic. You know that (seemingly harmless) thing we do? Where we compare every aspect of our lives to what's portrayed on social media? Our bodies, wardrobes, "momming" skills, houses, and vacations? Right here. I'm guilty. And true to glutton-for-punishment form, comparison was always my go-to vice. *Especially* on the days I felt like I was failing at life.

More often than not, my response to bad moments has been this: playing my life versus hers on social media. It's a habit, really. A toxic, damaging habit, but a habit just the same. My four-year-old seems to daily sabotage my every attempt at a clean, Joanna Gaines-approved house. My response? Instagram house lust starring the fabulous mother of two, who somehow has a spotless white couch and all things chippy white.

After a trying season of multiple miscarriages, being stuck in a job I hated, and living in a dreadful apartment, I found myself at it again. Sitting in my car on lunch break, I scrolled through pictures of the people I bitterly envied. Fabulous jobs. Easy pregnancies. Gorgeous houses. And then my moment of truth came. The weight of what I was doing hit me to my core. A gentle whisper resounded deep in my soul. *Nothing good will ever come from comparing your darkest days to someone else's brightest.* Nothing productive will ever come from comparison. Period.

The reality is, most people use social media as a series of "best of." Great moments. Flattering pictures. The best parts of our personal stories. Not the messy parts of life. And real life in all its fullness can't be compared. After my moment of revelation, I realized that I was using comparison as a means of personal punishment. The response to all my perceived shortcomings, flaws, and failures? Looking at pictures of what I believed my life should look like, while berating myself for not measuring up.

We are so incredibly unkind to ourselves sometimes. We pray for grace. We talk a great deal about grace. Yet we are so stingy with grace when it comes to extending it to ourselves. I believe to my core that God's grace is so far-reaching, it was meant to cover every aspect of our lives, even the most hidden parts of our hearts and minds where comparison thrives.

So these days you might say I'm a recovering compare-aholic. Life is unfolding–apart from the progress of the people I follow on social media. I'm learning to use the areas of my life that aren't ideal as a catalyst for change rather than a personal whipping post. I'm running my race with my eyes on my lane. Most of all, I'm learning how much a little dose of grace keeps comparison at bay.

When comparison tries to sneak in, we have a choice. We can dive into the destructive cycle of comparing/falling short/repeating. Or we can dive into grace. We can know the freedom that comes when we say no more comparison. No more my life versus anyone else's. Let's be women who say yes to grace.

Section Two

THE GRACE-FILLED LIFE

Chapter Six

ACCEPTED AND APPROVED

As long as we think we are not that bad, the idea of grace will never change us.

—Timothy Keller

Amazing grace. Grace that is greater than all our sins. By grace alone. I knew all about the word grace and how to use it properly in Christian circles, but I'll admit: I didn't really know what grace was until I hit my early thirties.

I have a strong sense of justice. I want things to be fair. You get what you deserve, and "God helps those who help themselves." I wrote in my first book about how grace opened my eyes to the fallacy in my thinking. I was a Pharisee who believed wrongly that the sins hidden in *my* heart were more acceptable because no one knew them. They weren't. Still aren't.

Grace gives us a compelling "He" reason to stop comparing while offering an irresistible invitation to start living. Grace mutes our stressed-out souls with the serenity of eternal security and quiets our fretful minds with the resolve to rest in him alone.

Grace fills that space between who we are and who we want to be. But make no mistake: grace is not a thing God grants us apart from himself. Instead, grace is God freely giving of himself for us.[1]

Grace literally means unmerited favor. We are chosen, forgiven, and then honored without any reason at all. It's really the opposite of fair. Once you start to see the world through the eyes of grace, you begin to notice just how much grace—unmerited favor—you've been shown. I love how Ephesians 4:7 defines grace in the Amplified version of the Bible: "Yet grace [God's undeserved favor] was given to each one of us [not indiscriminately, but in different ways] in proportion to the measure of Christ's [rich and abundant] gift."

After we've confessed our comparison struggles as sin, the filters of grace and gratitude can help us live out our lives comparison-free. In this section, we'll dive into four different types of grace that are all at work in the life of a believer: saving grace, sanctifying grace, growing grace, and sustaining grace. After exploring the fundamentals of grace, we'll examine how we can find freedom from comparison's grip by acknowledging the ways grace operates in our lives.

What It Means to Be Saved

One of the main reasons we compare ourselves to others is because of our longing for salvation. Sounds strange, right? But, inherently, we all crave salvation, and we all yearn for assurance that we're good enough to get it.

I bet you're not actually thinking about your salvation when you're envying the really fit woman racing on her treadmill at the gym or when you're browsing Pinterest and wondering why perfect mantel design seems easy for everyone else. But our understanding of saving grace may have more to do with our comparison struggles than you'd guess.

In case the concept of grace is new to you, I want you to have all the essential facts. Grace is a free gift that comes through believing in Jesus and acknowledging that we're sinners—hopeless in our ability to save ourselves. Timothy Keller explains it like this: we are more sinful than we could ever imagine but, through Christ, more loved than we could ever believe.

What does it *really* mean to be saved? Quite literally, it means to be rescued. Saving grace rescues us from the infectious fear, doubt, and insecurity that plague those who *don't* know their eternity rests solidly in the hands of almighty God. Salvation, in and of itself, offers enough grace to erase all of our mess. Yet God, in his infinite wisdom and love, gives us other manifestations of grace that help us change, grow, live, and endure.

We often breeze past this first type of grace. If you were raised in church, you may even take it for granted. (I know I did!) I didn't recognize how God's saving grace offers a firm foundation for my identity. Neither did I see how saving grace could impact the way I relate to others. God's saving grace frees us from fearing what others think, assuring us of our acceptance in him, which means God's saving grace offers us plenty of ammunition in our war against comparison. Salvation settles every question a comparing heart may ask. We only need to apply the answers.

Better Than We Deserve

When I was in tenth grade, a friend of my mom's won an all-expenses-paid trip for six to Walt Disney World. Her husband couldn't go along, and she had only one daughter, so she invited our family of four to join them.

We didn't fully understand what "all-expenses-paid" meant until we arrived in Orlando, where we stayed in a beautiful condominium and received free Disney park tickets. (Boy, could I use some of those now. *Sigh*. Disney admission times six? Yikes!) Plus, we ate free! Actually, "ate free" doesn't capture the magnitude of our food package. The tickets allowed for us *each* to partake of a free appetizer, entrée, beverage, and dessert at every meal in whatever restaurant we chose in the parks!

Five days (and fifteen pounds) later, we decided that "all-expenses-paid" was the only way to fully enjoy Disney World. (And I do mean fully!) Earning an all-expenses-paid vacation requires some connections, maybe even some merit—working hard enough at your sales job to earn a free trip, for example. But salvation doesn't require connections or commissions, only confession.

Max Lucado says it this way: "Confession is a radical reliance on grace. . . . 'What I did was bad,' we acknowledge, 'but your grace is greater than my sin, so I confess it.' If our understanding of grace is small, our confession will be small. . . . But great grace creates an honest confession."[2] If you've confessed your sins and accepted grace in return, you've been saved. There's no additional admission fee, and no way to earn it by being really awesome. Saving grace is as free as those Disney tickets. We didn't do anything to deserve a trip that fabulous, and yet, we were blessed with it.

Receiving this gift makes you a child of the King. Not just any head of state, but the King of Kings—Creator and Almighty God of the Universe (2 Cor. 6:18). Romans 8:39 tells us that nothing you can do will separate you from the love of God. You aren't just "special" like the characters on *Sesame Street* sang. You're legit royalty.

Yet we fight identity confusion every single day. We wonder if we're valuable on the days when our bloating is out of control and our hair won't behave. Will friends still like us when they see our outdated home? Will I have any friends at all if I don't go along with what everyone else is doing? Comparison adds to our identity confusion. According to our own measuring sticks, we fall short. We determine we're not enough. We can't keep up. But saving grace says that's not true, if we root our identity in Jesus.

Please understand the nuance here. I don't want to muddle the message of God's saving grace into self-esteem hype. If we meditate on our own "worthiness," we stay stuck in comparison's trap. We stop doing what we're supposed to do—reflect and give glory to God—and instead seek more glory for ourselves. (Remember this mantra: if you want to be free, the answer is never more of me.)

Saving grace tells us we're enough only because of what Jesus did for us. We measure up, according to God's standards, for this reason alone. We are nothing apart from him. Saving grace serves as a reminder of his splendor, not ours. To quote the apostle Paul, "By the grace of God, I am what I am" (1 Cor. 15:10). But feeling content with who and where I am? That's hard. My identity soars and sinks based on how I *feel* I'm doing. Too often, I fly high with perceived success or sink low with perceived failures. Finding the flat road down the middle—a steady state—feels impossible. I prefer to climb and crash.

In our culture, we retell the fable but often fail to recognize the tortoise who wins the race slow and steady. We prefer overnight successes. Rise to the top. Stand out from the crowd. Average might as well be reclassified as "not quite a winner." What if we spent more time thinking about how amazing it is that we've received God's unmerited favor and less time wondering if we're winning life's imaginary races? Could this not cure our comparison?

If my parents were leaving me ten million dollars when they pass, I don't think I'd stress over financial pressures now, even when money's tight. I could see a future hope for financial stability that would alleviate any current stress. Couldn't the same principles apply to the question of our worth? Could we actually be comfortable in our current state of "nothingness" knowing we've already inherited everything? Does how we feel now matter as much as what we'll experience for eternity?

My dad worked as an optometrist in private practice for most of my life. As a kid, I felt like a big shot entering that office. Even if the waiting room was full of patients, I strutted right through the white door that led to the exam rooms. If the door refused to open, I simply told the receptionist, "I'm here to see my dad." She unlocked it right away without question. I didn't need a seat in the waiting area. Neither did I need an appointment. Access was mine—any time I wanted. It's silly now, but I felt like a superstar. I assumed the waiting patients were jealous of me! I doubt anyone even noticed or cared, but convincing a nine-year-old girl that she wasn't special when she walked into her dad's office? Not a chance.

Friend, we've not only been rescued by the King of Kings, but we've been adopted. He's our dad. We have unlimited access to the throne of grace. We don't have to sit reading last month's *Family Circle* until we're called. He's already told us to come. All that he has is ours.

Your Identity Is Solid

"Let me know if you need me to go. I'm free that week."

The employee who's always willing to give 100 percent, that's me—especially when there's fun travel involved!

My boss was invited to speak to a group of wealthy contributors on a cruise ship. Though I offered in jest, a few weeks later, Larry asked me how I felt about babysitting. Seems his wife thought it'd be a good idea to take along a babysitter for their eighteen-month-old daughter. He suggested I go along to mingle with the affluent travelers during the day and to watch their daughter in the cabin after dinner so they could participate in the ship's nightlife. *So, wait. You're going to pay me to go on a cruise, and all I have to do is talk to people and babysit? I guess I can go. . . .*

A week before the ship left, he sweetened the deal. Larry stuck his head in my door to say I could take a friend along for no extra cost. "Find a friend who wants to go; then I'll have two babysitters." *I can do that.* It just so happened my friend Melissa was home from law school for the summer and lived just thirty minutes from the ship's New York City port. She happily hopped on the Bermuda bandwagon. (Or, in this case, cruise ship!)

Though we spent a lot of time babysitting, we were given generous pockets of free time to see and do things. We signed up for a Jet Ski adventure, thinking it'd be exhilarating to ride through the clear blue waters surrounding the island. The only trouble was, we didn't realize the excursion was a group tour—and the other members of our group happened to be eighteen-year-old boys determined to break the sound barrier on their ocean rockets. Melissa and I felt no need for that kind of speed. Our goal quickly became survival. Afraid of being lost at sea without our tour guide, we tried to keep up—at least enough so we could still see them.

Bad shifted into worse. The sky darkened as ominous clouds rolled in. After waiting for us to catch up, our tour leader circled the group to educate us on the severity of storms in Bermuda waters. We needed to head back immediately. "And, oh, by the way, make sure you keep the Jet Ski traveling faster than fifty miles per hour. As the water gets rougher, you could capsize unless you stay above the current. In this type of weather, you'll likely drown," he glibly explained. Listening stopped. Panic took over. Adrenaline chased fear through my every blood vessel. We were going to drown, get eaten by a shark, or be lost in the Bermuda Triangle forever—like Amelia Earhart. *They never found her remains.* I earnestly prayed, "God, please let us live. Please let us live."

I held the throttle while Melissa straddled behind me. She squeezed my chest so tight, air had no chance of traveling to my lungs. I mustered enough to shout, "Do you want to switch places?" She cried, "No. I just don't want to die!" (We're both a little dramatic.) After a frightening fifteen minutes, we spotted the shore again. We pulled those Jet Skis into the marina and fell to embrace the dry ground. I've never been happier to be on land.

Saving grace puts us on solid ground. We don't have to ride the waves of trying to keep up with trends or the neighbors. We're already accepted. No matter what we do, our footing stays sure. If storms come—or we fall behind and the tour group leaves us—saving grace assures us of our standing through Christ. Your identity is solid.

Max Lucado explains it in a beautiful way: "All of your fears of losing God's affection are needless. You can no more make him want you than you can convince him to abandon you. The adoption is irreversible. You have a place at his table."[3] Author Heather Holleman also writes about how being seated with Christ (Eph. 2:6) means we are free to drop out of the comparison game. We no longer have to keep trying to earn a seat at the "cool kids" table. A place has been set for us at the King's.[4]

Saving grace offers us the gospel in its simplest form. Many of us have this head knowledge, but what would our lives look like if we could really embrace this truth? If I wholeheartedly believed that I was accepted by God through Jesus and believed that Jesus loved me so much that he would die for me, why would I worry about being accepted by anyone else?

- If I truly kept a kingdom perspective—where I understood that this is just a temporary place, a temporary body, and a temporary condition—why would I fixate on the digital readout from a box on the bathroom floor or a possible dirty look from a colleague?
- If I were able to fully understand, grasp, and comprehend God's love for me, would I ever have cause to feel unworthy and compare myself to others?

- If I could just grasp the magnitude of God the Creator in relation to me, the creation, I would have no reason to be afraid of what others think of my legs, my lawn, or my life. God loves me. Why does anyone else's opinion matter?

If I could understand the enormous saving grace of God and believe it, all the areas where comparison tries to stress me out—from swimsuit season to standardized test scores—wouldn't really matter very much. Would they?

Takeaway

Saving grace is what we receive at the moment of salvation. It's a free gift; we can't earn or attempt to pay for it. Saving grace cures comparison by securing our identity, reminding us that we are loved no matter how we measure up to others. We have unlimited access to the throne and a seat at the King's table, through grace and not by our own merit.

Comparison-Free Life Action Plan

Look up the passages referenced in this chapter: Ephesians 4:7, Romans 8:39, 2 Corinthians 6:18, and 1 Corinthians 15:10. Also read Philippians 2. List ten things you learn about our identity and God's grace from these passages.

1. Do you view salvation as your rescue? Why or why not?

2. In what ways has a life of comparison impacted your identity? In what ways do you think saving grace could solidify it?

3. "If I wholeheartedly believed that I am accepted by God through Jesus and believed that Jesus loves me so much that he would die for me, why would I worry about being accepted by anyone else?" Does this question resonate with you? Do you believe this kind of assurance is reasonable?

4. What does it mean to you that, if you're saved, you've been adopted by Christ and have a seat at his table? What does this make you think of?

Memory Verse: "But by the grace of God I am what I am, and his grace toward me was not in vain. On the contrary, I worked harder than any of them, though it was not I, but the grace of God that is with me" (1 Cor. 15:10).

Lord, please give me fresh eyes to understand your saving grace in a way that applies to every area of my heart and mind. Show me how my worthiness and identity can be firmly rooted in you alone. Thank you for the sacrifice of your Son that made this saving grace possible. In Jesus's name, Amen.

Chapter Seven

GRACE ALLEVIATES OUR FEARS

Our greatest fear should not be of failure, but of succeeding at something that doesn't really matter.

–Dwight L. Moody

Speaking of the "cool kids" table, can I confess something? I really believed all that peer pressure and social stratification would disappear after high school. After college at the latest. Boy, was I wrong. (Thank you, Facebook.)

But, like me, you may remember how trying to be part of the "in crowd" came with a lot of pressure. Were my jeans the "right" brand? Did my bangs possess enough poof? (In the late eighties, the answer was always no. They could always be higher.) Could I sound "cool" when I talked? Did I know enough about the hottest music and movies? (I wasn't allowed to listen to rock music or watch most movies. Sounding like I was "in the know" required secret study!) Plus, I sweat when I get nervous. Just being around the cool kids practically required stuffing tissues in my armpits. When those oversized silk blouses were popular, I had real struggles. (Yes, we're back to talking about sweating.)

As I look back on those days and years of striving to fit in, I see something I couldn't have aptly named for you as a teen or even a twenty-something. It's called fear. Fear told me I wouldn't be accepted. Fear told me I'd never be enough—and it was preposterous for me to believe I could ever be more. "You'll never be anyone's first choice," Fear whispered. "You'll never be worthy of love." The truth is that fear still lies to me all the time. Maybe it lies to you too?

But saving grace sings a different song. Saving grace

- releases us from the shackles of fear;
- topples our idols of perfection, work, and approval; and
- frees us from a scarcity mentality.

Wow! As you read that list, I wonder if you're thinking, *Really? Saving grace does all that?* But it does, my friend. Allow me to show you how.

Fear

F-E-A-R. Four letters that dominated my life too often. If you're a bit of a security freak like me, you've likely felt it too. Fear told me it's a big scary monster that's going to swallow me whole. Sometimes I believed it. I trembled and cowered—fearing the opinions of others, fearing the worst in every unclear circumstance. I assigned motives to the innocent or blindly followed the guilty because everyone else did. I missed my purpose and surrendered my freedom.

There's an answer to fear's scary "You'll never win!" sneers. Saving grace responds, "You've already won!" Then it shines a bright light on fear's shadow until it disappears. Seriously, if God can take care of our sin problem, is there anything he's not big enough to handle?

Scripture tells us over and again not to fear, but we find it easy to ignore those commands. Fear not? *Sounds impossible.* I'm editing this book in the midst of the COVID-19 quarantine with no idea what grim news tomorrow will bring. Every time I scroll the Internet, I'm offered a plethora of reasons to fear. Child abduction at the grocery store? Human traffickers at gas stations? Corporate layoffs? Hackers stealing my passwords? EF-5 tornados? Can God really expect me not to fear when invisible germs are everywhere and danger lurks in empty parking lots and email attachments? The answer is yes.

On any given day, our biggest fears can range from what others think of our outfits to whether or not our children will ever find a job and leave home. But David offers this reminder in Psalm 27:1: "The LORD is my light and my salvation; whom shall I fear? The LORD is the stronghold of my life; of whom shall I be afraid?"

Friend, God's saving grace says you have no reason to fear. He's got you. You can rest secure in him because he's omnipotent—not just strong, but all-powerful. We see his strength most in areas where we're weak. When comparison causes those weaknesses to drift into feelings of doubt or self-loathing, recognize it and call it by name. Say, "Fear, you're not welcome here. Saving grace took care of you."

The Idol of Perfection

As an intern in college, I worked in the communications office. Our group created an annual report to update donors and alumni on the school's activities. Publishing this booklet required *a lot* of effort on the part of the staff, so when the boxes of finished books arrived fresh from the printer, my boss couldn't wait to crack them open. The smell of fresh ink permeated the room as he distributed copies for all to admire. We flipped through the color pictures, praising the way the finished product turned out.

That is, until the office secretary noticed a typo. One little letter was missing from a word, but it was a significant omission. The word public was missing an "l." And trust me, that "l" is one you don't want to leave out, lest you change your meaning significantly. Worst of all, the error wasn't hidden on page thirty. It was in the very first line of the first page. It was a perfectionist's worst nightmare. I felt guilt and shame over that mistake. Sure, I'd proofread the book. But so did several others. I was only an intern, not even close to being responsible for the finished product. Yet my perfectionist's heart kept an error log.

There's a special section in my brain that stores my mistakes. Every misstep or misspeak—they're all recorded and played back to me as reminders of my inadequacy. For decades, I felt bound by this perfectionism. I wanted everyone to believe I had it all together. If you came to my house, it looked spotless. If you ran into me at Target, I wore an actual outfit and makeup. I even tried on different workout ensembles before going to the gym. That's how image-focused I was. Candidly, it was all just fear. But the filter of grace removed those shackles of perfection. God's saving grace sets the perfectionist free with the truth that we'll never be good enough to bridge our own chasm. Only his grace is enough. Being good enough—as close to perfect as we can muster—still leaves us short.

On the other hand, culturally we've made a new idol out of being imperfect. And while as believers we need to accept our own brokenness in order to receive God's grace, we must be careful not to glorify it. Instagram presents a gallery of carefully curated "realness," while transparency and authenticity have turned into buzzwords. We've been told to label our mess as "beautiful," creating an obscure new standard of muddled perfection. We pick and choose what areas to (secretly) strive in, then lump the rest of our mess in a big "being authentic" box. We work hard to get the perfect makeup-free selfie, looking disheveled, so everyone will know we're real. It's still perfectionism. Only now we have to be some weird type of perfectly imperfect. What's worse is that we boast in our mediocrity. Greatness is overrated—that's for the perfect ones, and "we don't like them."

Idolizing imperfection hasn't freed anyone. There's still too much emphasis on us—our performance and meeting a certain standard of acceptability. Praising ourselves for being average instead of awesome is still misplaced worship. Our mess isn't beautiful: what's beautiful is how Jesus showers us with redemptive grace despite how messy we are.

Perfect is the enemy of sanctified. Unless you're willing to identify your idols, you'll stay enslaved to them. The charade of perfection removes the prescription lenses of God's sanctifying grace, and with a blind eye says, "Thanks for the salvation, God. I've got it from here."

Perfectionism snubs the gospel. Its mantra touts the attainability of righteousness. With a little more hard effort, I can get everything right and become worthy on my own merit. *Uh. No, friend. You can't.* That's just more idolatry, and it's going to keep you out of the life of grace.

The perfectionist thinks, "I'll get the perfect body, then they will love me."

The gospel says, "I love you no matter what size you are. Jesus's death means your physical appearance no longer determines your worth."

The perfectionist thinks, "I want everyone to know what a good homemaker I am. My spotless house will smell like banana bread, even if you're only stopping by for a minute."

The gospel says, "Jesus died so that you could be free from the pressure of what others think of you."

The perfectionist enjoys being right, driving the cleanest car, maintaining the greenest lawn, and having her children impeccably dressed—out of a desire to prove her worth. It's self-justification. And it's the opposite of the gospel. Deep down, the perfectionist fears that she's not enough, that she's not accepted, or that she can't relax for a second or she'll lose comparison's game. Hidden fear drives perfectionism. Only saving grace can settle the perfectionist's heart.

The Idol of Work

The music blares as we reach one of the most intense parts of the workout. With resistance set high, I encourage my spin class as they climb to the top of an imaginary hill. "Picture Everest!" I yell. "Come on . . . WORK FOR IT!" Sure, I threw in "You can do it" and an occasional "Don't give up!" throughout the ride, but "Work for it!" was my go-to cheer when I sensed struggle. If sweat soaked their handlebars and legs began to slow, I coached them to keep working so they could *earn* their results.

My exercise philosophy during the years I taught indoor cycling classes wasn't unusual. You only get out what you put in, right? You turn that knob, fight for every pedal stroke, and make your muscles beg you to stop. As a reward for your effort, in weeks or months, you'll see a difference. Then you'll be entitled to whatever results you've earned. Ironically, after a decade on that spin bike, my own "working for it" took a toll on my body. My adrenal system tired, and challenging cardio now renders me useless for days. I've been forced to reconsider what I believe about exercise . . . and life.

"Work for it" wasn't just my motto in the spin room. It was a subtle yet driving principle in my worldview. I like to work. My natural inclination is to work for God's love, to perform well so that he will love me more. *Look at the rules I followed so well, God.* I want to work for it, and I want to be perfect at it. Then, in the economy of my flesh, I get good because I *deserve* good. But this equation conspicuously lacks something I claim to believe and accept: grace. The concept that God can't love me any more than he does right now is difficult for my feeble mind to digest. Compound that with the fact that he can't love me any less. Mind. Blown.

If I don't consider God's love and salvation through faith in Christ Jesus a free gift, then I wind up trying to save myself through my work. I dismiss the gift.

For example, I have a difficult time receiving presents. If you went out and bought me something fabulous, I'd probably feel uncomfortable. Alternatively, if I watched your children for a week, cleaned your house, and/or counseled you through your body image issues and you surprised me with a cute purse, I might be okay with that. But God's not looking for my contribution to his effort. He wants me to see how the work was finished on the cross.

If I can't earn it, then what's a worker bee to do? We need to put aside our work-for-it mentality. It may feel contrary to everything within you. It's countercultural to believe that you're justified, accepted, and "enough" without contributing your best. Instagram ads tell me I must hustle to succeed. Life coaches tell me I'll rest after I earn my own way. Then, the voice of comparison tells me I can't let up or others will get ahead of me.

Galatians 6:4 encourages us to test our own work, while 2 Timothy 2:15 reminds us to present ourselves to God as a worker who has no need to be ashamed. It's not that God doesn't expect us to work. (Faith without works is dead, after all; see James 2:14–26.) But we do have to check our hearts. Why are we working? Are we deriving identity from our work? Are we working as unto the Lord, or are we chasing idols like money, success, fame, or status? We don't have to overwork. Our identities are secure, even when our success doesn't look like we hoped it would.

"Working for it" is not the message of the gospel. The yoke of Jesus is easy and his burden is light. Saving grace says your identity is separate from your work.

The Idol of Approval

Securing our identities in Christ topples those idols of "I need everyone to like me," or "I want everyone to think I'm pretty." Other self-obsessed thoughts, like "I hope they all think I'm a good mom" or "I hope other women at church see me as good Christian," fall too. Acceptance leads us to a place where we no longer need anyone's stamp of approval aside from God's. Fully comprehending Christ's acceptance offers relief for our social anxiety too. We no longer need to stress over what others think of us, what they will say to us, or how they will treat us.

Resting in God's saving grace secures our identities so we can let go of our expectations—those often-unrealistic standards we try to live up to. (Remember Paul's example from 1 Corinthians 4:3, in which he refused to judge himself.) When we reach this level of confidence in Christ's love and grace for us:

- It becomes okay to show up at small group with store-bought cupcakes. You're already accepted.
- It no longer feels like a crushing blow when someone doesn't recognize how hard you worked on that presentation. You're already accepted.
- It doesn't matter if every other mom picked up her child from practice on time and you're running ten minutes late. You don't have to beat yourself up over whether or not coach thinks you're a horrible mother. (Hypothetically speaking, of course.) You're already accepted.

I wonder how much better we'd all get along if we could believe this. Even if we could get this right as the church, what a difference we could make. When we don't believe that we're fully accepted, we struggle to accept others. But in the life of grace, there's no place for pride, bias, or stereotypes. Our unmerited acceptance through Christ's saving grace means we have no excuse not to offer that same level of acceptance of others, no matter how different they are.

Several years ago, I changed my ministry's name to "Compared to Who?" Consequently, I'm more content than ever to go without makeup. (I have no evidence of actual correlation, but I think this is true.) I can sit in Starbucks writing while wearing my "Compared to Who?" shirt with workout pants, Crocs, and crazy hair. Most days, I'm not afraid of what anyone thinks of my appearance. But when it comes to what others think about my character? *Ouch!* Fear of man swells bigger than my ankles did during the July I was nine months pregnant. I care what you think of me. I want you to think I'm nice. I have a "being liked by everyone" idol that I must regularly deconstruct.

Because God is gracious enough to bring these things to light, he allowed me an opportunity to explore my struggle with fear of man. A disagreement surfaced in our little church. Words were twisted. Sides were rallied. Hurt feelings lead to hurtful words and, somehow, I looked like one of the bad guys. Discouragement and frustration made me feel uncomfortable and heavy, like wearing a scratchy wool sweater in the summer. I wanted any insinuation of me being "not nice" gone. Stat. I didn't know what to do. So I resorted to tactics that anyone who'd spent a dozen years working in public relations and politics would use when faced with a similar situation: I tried to control the spin. *Perhaps I could talk to people in the middle so they could see there are two sides to the story.*

Do you know what happened? It didn't work. *At all.* In fact, I got myself into a heap of trouble, as defending myself led to repeating secret things I knew but had no business telling anyone else. I inadvertently gossiped to try to stop a gossip. It made the mess even worse. Women I once deemed good friends shut me out in an instant. Today I live with a reality that I hate. There are some women who still don't like me. They've never heard my side of the story, but they believe I acted both unkindly and unjustly. *Ugh.* It sickens me. I was unfriended in real life and on Facebook (which, in some bizarre way, is almost worse than just being unfriended in real life).

As I continue to learn to rely on the truth of Scripture, I see that Jesus was misunderstood, despised, and rejected. *Rejected. Yikes. No one likes rejection. Anything but that.* There's a good chance Jesus would have been blocked on social media too, though unlike me, Jesus did nothing to deserve it. We know people said mean and untrue things behind his back. Scripture tells us that everything we experience here, he also experienced (Heb. 4:15). The sooner I learn there's no way to make everyone like me, the better. In fact, if I'm making everyone happy, there's a good chance I'm not following Christ.

What if we believed that even death can't defeat us? What then would we have to be afraid of? Gossips? Bullies? Cool kids who act like you're stupid because you don't wear the right brand of shoes?

Saving grace defeats fear of people. It can also defeat that oppressor in our heads. Let's be honest: Most of what we wrestle isn't other people saying mean things to our faces. Instead, it's what we *believe* they're thinking that berates us. Sometimes, this is more severe than if we'd actually heard their condemnation. You see, I don't need you to *actually* say anything bad about me. I'm "talented" enough to create *for you* a list of things you probably don't like about me. Then, in my head, I will convince myself that

I must improve so *you* can let go of the list and return to liking me. Yes, I can do all of this without you saying a word! What you actually think of me doesn't matter. The oppressor keeps me busy reading *his* lies into *your* every action.

Why do we get stuck in fear of people? Could it be we're building our identity more on our good reputation than on Jesus? Maybe we want to believe we're more important than we actually are? Anyone who dares imply otherwise topples our ego like a tower of plastic blocks.

Yes, we should strive to walk with godly character and to live "beyond reproach." My goal has been to behave in such a way that when someone falsely accuses me, others would say, "That's so odd. I really don't think that's consistent with what I know of her." But it won't always work that way. I learned that the hard way when a handful of women who shouldn't have been involved were happy to take the other side in our church conflict. It hurt and confused me. I thought, "If only they knew the whole truth."

But maybe that wouldn't have made it better. My friend and pastor's wife Cindy told me the story of how she endured a similar situation. She prayed, "God, if they only knew my heart." And God reminded her, "If they only knew your heart, they'd have many more reasons not to like you." *Wow!* Message received. It's pride that tells us we're anything other than saints who sin and need grace. It's pride that wants us to build identity on our "niceness." And it's pride that fools us into believing that it's okay to keep that approval idol.

Rest and resolution can only be found in God's saving grace. I confess any sin I know I committed and then try to ignore the rest of the drama. Only God's saving grace affords me unmerited favor. What others think of me doesn't increase my admission price—Jesus already suffered the cost. There's no way for me to "help" him pay. To think I make it easier for him to save me because

I'm popular, accepted by everyone, or "nice" sounds as foolish as it is. My hope isn't found in unconditional acceptance from both strangers and friends; my hope is that someday God will tell me, "Well done, my daughter. You've been faithful." As 1 Peter 1:13 instructs, "Set your hope fully on the grace that will be brought to you at the revelation of Jesus Christ." His grace saves me for eternity. If I can remember this truth now, I loosen the grip comparison holds on my life because of fear of man (or woman!).

God recently showed me another important lesson about my need for approval. Friends of ours adopted a beautiful goldendoodle. When Lucy, a talented service dog, sees a bag of treats, do you know what she does? Every trick she knows. Lucy will roll over, shake, sit . . . sometimes all three at once. She's so desperate for her doggy cookie, she'll keep cycling through her trick repertoire until the reward is delivered. As I watched Lucy, I recognized how much I'm just like her. My approval idol kept me that way. What kind of Heather would you like? Oh, you wanted me to be nicer? Sure, I could do that. Thinner? Yep, I had a whole list of unhealthy tricks to attempt that too. Would you love me more if I were smarter, quieter, or less opinionated? I would perform. Anything for that treat of your approval. Anything! *Did I do it well enough? Do you like me? Can I have my treat now?* (pant pant).

Have you played approval's game too? God's saving grace frees us from all types of performance. We don't have to do anything to earn his love and acceptance. But we do have to give up our desire for approval. We can't live for both Jesus and the approval of others. That approval idol has to go. My approval comes from Christ alone.

Scarcity Mentality

By age seven, I knew exactly what career I wanted. My parents got a new washing machine, and I cut a giant rectangular hole into the front of the box. Though it took some finagling, I found a way to stand inside that box and dress rehearse my life's dream. "Good evening. This is *NBC Nightly News*. First up tonight . . ."

In high school, I did the morning announcements. On career day, I shadowed local broadcasters. I wanted nothing more than to be an anchorwoman. But in my first year of college, I made the decision not to pursue a career in broadcast journalism. Why? There were too many people in my freshman communications course who held the same ambition. If we all wanted the same thing, there would be no room for me. I quickly added a second major and decided maybe politics or marketing would be a better fit. Less competition. Yes, I said the "c" word.

We're comfortable talking about comparison as comparison, but what about comparison as competition? Though slightly nuanced, it's scarcity mentality that takes something harmful (comparison) and turns it into something even more damaging. I'm not sure how or why my thinking always revolved around competition, but it did. *Always.* Sometimes it still does. I like to win. I prefer situations where I know I can win. If I assess a particular climate as a place I'll never succeed, I move on.

This thinking almost ended my writing career before it got started! Time and again those voices in my head told me that the world doesn't need another woman talking about this issue. "You don't have anything to add." "You don't write very well." "No one cares about the words you say." These thoughts persuaded me, almost daily, to just give up. Then I remembered studying the scarcity mentality. It's a concept from Stephen Covey's *The 7 Habits of Highly Effective People*—a book I read with my team as a manager almost twenty years ago. *Could this apply to my writing? My body image? My spiritual gifts? My envy?*

In order to understand this concept, first picture a pie. (Whatever kind you like best—fruit or pizza!) With scarcity mentality, one believes that because there's a limited amount of pie, the slices are numbered. With every slice claimed, there will be less, or possibly none, left for you. Everything is limited. Life is a sort of *Hunger Games* competition for each slice. Compete well or no pie for you.

I knew this was my problem. As I continued to compare myself to other writers, I felt like they were getting "all" of the book contracts, they had "all" of the readers, or they filled "all" the speaking spots for Christian women. But God has given us each a voice. Even if two women have the same message, they'll still say it in a different way based on their own experiences, background, and story. In other words, there's plenty of pie for everyone.

I also held a scarcity mentality in the area of body image. Somehow, twisted in my mind, I believed that there was only room for one "type" of beautiful woman. I heard people speak of beauty in other cultures, or different styles of beauty, but those concepts never resonated. There's only one I recognized—the one you see on TV or in magazines. Stick thin. Gorgeous hair. Flawless skin. Curves in all the right places. In my scarcity mentality, I didn't think there was room for me to be considered beautiful unless I met those criteria. This world didn't have enough space to accept more than one definition of physical beauty. I made this my idol and secretly committed myself to attaining it.

The opposite of the scarcity mentality is the abundance mentality. Covey believes you can only develop this type of outlook if you have a strong sense of personal worth.[1] I'd argue that you can have an abundance mentality when you know, securely, who you are thanks to God's saving grace. With an abundance mentality, you can look at life through the lens of plenty, not as a competition.

How would our struggles with comparison change if we lived with an abundance mentality? What if we truly believed it was okay for us all to be beautiful in different ways—even if they aren't the ways the magazines tout as beautiful? What if we didn't feel threatened by others' gifts because we knew the God of the universe had a designated place for us to use ours?

Saving grace assures us that we have all we need through Jesus. There's no need to compete, compare, or worry about there being enough pie. In fact, instead of envy and jealousy, we find ourselves content enough to encourage each other . . . and maybe even share a slice.

Takeaway

Saving grace is part of God's free gift of salvation. It frees us from comparison because it releases us from the burden of fear, anxiety, and stress. We no longer have to compare ourselves to others and worry we fall short. We no longer have to "work for it" or feel the pressure of perfectionism. We can rest in God's abundance.

Comparison-Free Life Action Plan

Read Psalm 27:1 and 1 Peter 1:13, both referenced in this chapter, as well as these other verses: Deuteronomy 3:18, Isaiah 43:1, Psalm 18:2, John 14:27, and Joshua 1:9. There are between 300 and 365 uses of the words fear and afraid in the Bible. Why do you think God addresses fear so frequently? How do you believe God wants us to handle our fear? What brings you the most comfort when you confront fear personally?

1. In what areas of your life do you long for (or feel you need) the approval of others? How can God's saving grace help you defeat the idol of approval?

2. Do you ever feel tempted to "work for it"? What messages from culture have you heard about earning what we deserve? How does this message differ from God's message of saving grace?

3. Have you ever wrestled perfectionism? How does God's saving grace speak to fear and perfectionism?

4. In what areas of your life have you held a scarcity mentality, believing there was a limited amount of God's provision or a limited need for your gifts in the kingdom?

Memory Verse: "There is no fear in love, but perfect love casts out fear. For fear has to do with punishment, and whoever fears has not been perfected in love" (1 John 4:18).

Heavenly Father, free me from the bondage of perfectionism and approval. Show me that there's nothing I can do to add to your free gift of saving grace. Help me to understand that you've set me free from all fear. Show me how to live freely in the truth that you have a place and a purpose for me. Amen.

Chapter Eight

GOD GIVES GREAT MAKEOVERS

My soul is like a house, small for you to enter,
but I pray you to enlarge it.
It is in ruins, but I ask you to remake it.
It contains much that you will not be pleased
to see: this I know and do not hide.
But who is to rid it of these things?
There is no one but you.

–Augustine of Hippo, *Confessions*

Put a metal bucket over your head, then ask nearby children to scream up into it, and you'll get an accurate feel for my writing conditions today. This hotel has an indoor pool. *Great! I'll get lots done while the children swim.* How wrong I was. This is not a vacation. This is torture.

Kauai. Now *that* was a vacation. We spent ten days there for our honeymoon. Gorgeous sunsets, pristine beaches, a lovely hotel room, floral leis draped around our necks . . . and I was miserable. *I bet you didn't expect me to say that.* See, it was my husband's fault, really. He didn't know that honeymoons meant sleeping till noon and eating meals from the room service menu. Instead, he was up at five A.M., saying, "Let's beat the rush to the breakfast buffet!" *What?*

As if leaving the hotel room wasn't bad enough, he wanted us to do activities—like hiking through rainforests, climbing canyons, and riding in helicopters without doors. They filmed *Jurassic Park* on the island, if that helps you picture the terrain. *Who was this outdoorsy man, and how did I end up married to him?* My idea of vacation includes the following: a lounge chair, a stack of books, and a bright-pink fruity drink with an umbrella. I define outdoorsy as choosing the patio pool *over* the indoor one. When I get tired of lying in the sun, I move on to my next favorite vacation activity—shopping. Follow that with a nice dinner and a sampling of local ice cream parlors, and you'll create my perfect getaway.

But this was not my honeymoon. By the sixth day of jungle trekking, I felt a mix of anger and disappointment. I hadn't seen the inside of a single gift shop and didn't know the quickest route to the pool. I couldn't take it any longer. My CDD (chronic disappointment disorder) flared. I had but one option: start a fight with my new husband about how our honeymoon was "all wrong," and it was all his fault.

In the months leading up to our wedding, I read *Sacred Marriage* by Gary Thomas. Internally, I bristled at his thesis. God cares more about my holiness than my happiness? *Are you kidding, Gary? Marriage will make me happier than anything else in this world. If I wanted to be holier, I'd join a convent.* Turns out, Gary was right. Marriage proved a giant exercise in sanctification—right from the start. When I was single, my selfishness stayed hidden. But, with a ring on my finger, it glared too brightly to miss.

When life gets hard, and its lessons feel like the test we forgot to study for, we should count it all grace. Sure, in the midst of

God's schooling, I'd prefer to call it a lot of other things. I name my lessons "struggles" or "trials." I've even called them "the enemy messing with my life." But, it's often sanctification. God reveals things in our character that keep us from his heart. Apparently, the only way to learn these lessons is to actually experience them. (Can't I just take the online class?)

Sanctification doesn't always feel like grace. Some days it feels like heartache (or a disappointing honeymoon!). But if we can see our biggest earthly struggles as part of this sanctification process, that's good news for our comparison battle.

What Is Sanctifying Grace?

I don't remember a lot from my children's baby days—I birthed four children in just over four years and it's a blur—but I do remember entertaining games of hide-and-seek. The bigger kids would choose legitimate places to hide, like under a desk or in the pantry. But my younger boys would often just bury their faces under the pillows on the couch, backsides fully exposed. As a cute, squishy rear end protruded from the cushions, I'd hear the delighted giggles of a child convinced he was out of sight. When a "seeker" entered the room and said, "Where'd Trevor go?" Trevor, my middle son, would pull the pillow off and flash a cheeky grin, proud of how well he'd hidden.

Sanctification reveals all the ridiculous places we try to hide. He calls us to grow up and, as Psalm 32:7 says, find a safer hiding place. I wonder if God doesn't look down as we try to cover our shame with pillows and think, "My child, you have no idea how exposed you are hiding there."

I've buried my nose in a lot of insufficient shelters. Maybe you can relate? I thought that having a better body would be the "protection" I needed against rejection. When that didn't work, I'd hide in food—eating for comfort and security, not sustenance.

I've hidden in my work too, believing that success would certainly lead to respect. (I'm super good at this one!) Approval from others, dating relationships, exercise, pride, and self-pity—these proved to be hiding places that offered no protection when life's chaos made me a target. All my hiding is really just idolatry.

When Timothy Keller preaches about sanctification, he talks about how it reveals the idols of the heart. Author Paul David Tripp further clarifies the role of sanctifying grace like this: "We want our lives to be comfortable, successful, and predictable, but God is willing to compromise all of these in order to deal with our deepest difficulty: indwelling and remaining sin."[1] I like to think about sanctification as God's makeover stories. But, unlike the transformations that occur on *Extreme Makeover: Home Edition* or *The Biggest Loser*, God changes us from the inside out. He takes our hearts of stone and turns them to flesh (Ezek. 36:26). He gradually and graciously shows us where we need to change for our good and his glory.

God's greatest desire is not that we live in a *Property Brothers* decorated home, with size-six clothes in our closet, five thousand Instagram followers, and a BMW in the garage. These earthly measures of success can't compare to God's dreams for our lives. Instead, God wants us to look more like Jesus. You know, his "man of sorrows," homeless Son who was betrayed by his friends and rejected in every way imaginable. *Yikes.*

I remember a pastor asking the question, "Is this really what you signed up for?" If you examine the life of Jesus or the apostles, words like comfortable, easy, or fabulous never come to mind. John Piper once said, "If God's love for his children is to be measured by our health, wealth, and comfort in this life, God hated the apostle Paul." That's jarring, isn't it? But sanctification can change our perspective *and* our vision boards.

After God's saving grace opens our spiritually blind eyes (John 14:17–20), God's sanctifying grace gives us the proper prescription to see our sins with greater clarity. This makes it easier to stop falling victim to each of comparison's cons. Author Stephen Altrogge nails it here: "If the gospel brought forgiveness of sins but didn't give power over sins, it would seem like a cheap trick. After all, what good would it be if our idolatry was forgiven but we still lusted after every shiny thing that crossed our path?"[2]

As we examine sanctification, we'll first look at the ways God helps us see idols clearly. Then, we'll explore how God's sanctifying grace frees us from striving for perfection. Finally, we'll look at the ways sanctification can change our perspective so we can stop comparing our journeys and start living on purpose.

Seeing Idols Clearly

Every time sanctification's paintbrush sweeps by me, I'm forced to answer this question: Is Jesus enough? You see, in the life of comparison, idols rule. They dictate our mood for the day or how many hours we work (in the gym or the office). They, too often, run our lives—subconsciously affecting everything from how we treat our children to what we post on social media to why we get angry with our husbands. But God's sanctifying grace helps us recognize our idols, call them out, repent, and repeat.

Yes, repeat! Not like lather, rinse, repeat. You don't have to do it twice like some silly formula that just wastes shampoo. Instead, my friend, we must recognize that idols are sneaky. They will pester us all day, every day, unless we consistently identify them and then change the posture of our lives to one of continuous repentance. Idols grip our hands and pull us down pride's path, telling us that we're right and everyone else is wrong. That's why I get nervous when I hear women say they're going to stop apologizing.

Repentance is vital to our connection with Jesus; a humble heart supplies the oxygen for healthy relationships with others.

How do you see idols clearly? To spot a counterfeit, you must first know the real thing. This reminds me of when I lived in Washington, D.C. Daily I'd walk by the street vendors selling "designer" purses and, truth is, I couldn't tell they were fake. Since I didn't make enough money to afford a real Prada purse, I bought one for $20 outside a metro stop. I'd never even touched an authentic Prada, so this bag seemed amazing to me. It wasn't until my purse aficionado roommate pointed out that I'd bought a "Prado" instead of a "Prada" that I felt a little cheated.

When we recognize Jesus as our true source of satisfaction, it's easier to spot idols. The more you get to know him—his love, his grace, even the Holy Spirit's conviction—the easier it is to see the deficiencies of idols in all of these arenas. Spending time in his Word, praying daily to deepen your relationship, and sitting under solid biblical teaching every week will help you recognize the only authentic savior. Sanctification requires this diligence.

The second way to see idols clearly is to be in community. Notice I separated church attendance from "being in community." Just showing up on Sunday is not the same as having people who know and love you, who can and will speak into your life. Small groups, discipleship groups, mentor relationships, and even close Christian friendships can offer you an opportunity to grow in sanctification alongside others. Letting others into your life in an intentional way gives idols hiding in our blind spots the opportunity to come to the light.

Finally, while listening to the conviction of the Holy Spirit and receiving helpful counsel from friends, make your own list of potential idols by answering the following questions:

- What do I spend most of my time thinking about or "obsessing" over?
- What do I fear losing the most?
- Where does the majority of my time and money go?
- Which goals and dreams consume me?
- What do I lose my temper over the most?

Write your answers on an index card and pray daily for God to help tear down all the idols you see and, through his sanctifying grace, reveal any that remain hidden. As you make your list remember that God is not a harsh schoolteacher looking for us to step out of line so he can issue demerits. It's an extreme act of love for God to show us sin that lingers in our lives. He knows the consequences of our idolatry. Like a good father, he tries to protect us from its entrapment. Sanctification is a gift.

We're All Imperfect

As we continue to examine God's sanctifying grace, let's all acknowledge this truth: No one is already perfect. I know you *know* that. But does your heart believe it? Sometimes it's easy to quietly chase perfection while hashtagging our own missteps with "Nobody's perfect!" We talked about how the idol of perfectionism snubs God's saving grace. Now, let's examine the dissonance between sanctification and perfectionism.

A group of moms sat around the table, stealing bites of lunch in between feeding babies and punching holes in juice boxes. The discussion turned to minivans and how, when you spend a lot of time shuttling kids, they become trash cans on wheels. I nodded and smiled, understanding exactly what they meant, until her comment jarred me.

"Of course, the Creekmores' van doesn't look like that."

Uh, what? Completely caught off guard, I replied, "It sure does! I just have a husband who cleans it regularly for his own sanity. If it were left up to me, who knows what condition that thing would be in?"

"You just have to be perfect at everything, don't you?" she sneered.

I didn't know what else to say. I'm nowhere close to being perfect. Listening to just one episode of my podcast would reveal that even after decades of sanctification, I still have many struggles. But then it clicked. I saw how longing for perfection on earth actually precludes us from embracing God's sanctifying grace. Since the fall of man in Genesis, there's been no such thing as perfection here on earth. We must replace our strivings for this type of perfection with a desire for holiness. If we don't, chasing earthly perfection will keep us comparing ourselves to others instead of praying for God to make us more like Jesus.

My friend Lauren's aunt worked for a major food company when they were trying to make a tastier reduced-fat cream cheese. The product development team kept comparing each progressive version of the product to the previous version, instead of comparing it to actual cream cheese. Several iterations later, it didn't taste anything like the original. Friend, this is what happens when we compare ourselves to anyone other than Jesus. "Bettering" our lives based on what and who we see around us won't lead us to perfection. Instead, it may be a sure-fire way to create a fake. God wants us only to pursue and replicate the original.

Sometimes the desire for perfection can reveal an unusual idol—the idol of self. We (secretly) desire perfection because of the applause it would bring. But here's some sobering food for thought. Satan was dismissed from heaven for his vanity. He didn't want to bask in God's glory; he craved his own. Now he lures us with this same sin. Our flesh desires to stand out—"Be all you can be!" and "You do you!" Meanwhile, God tells us that he'll keep us safe if we stay under his wings. Psalm 63:7 reminds us that contentment and joy are found in God's shadow, not in the spotlight.

If you've ever struggled even for a day with striving for perfection, the thought of having your weaknesses brought to the light may sound stressful. But let me encourage you: Jesus doesn't expect us to take a single step alone. His sanctification is never a risky and shameful unveiling. Instead, the gospel covers us, completely. He's a sufficient shelter.

We Can't Compare Journeys

Our family loves to watch the *Amazing Race* on television. This has to be the forty-fifth season or something like that. I hope they never cancel the show. We each choose and cheer for our favorite teams. My husband, Eric, roots for anyone former military, while our daughter picks the all-girl team. I prefer the couples that seem to have a good on-camera relationship, while our sons latch on to anyone in the lead.

Eric and I thought about trying out a few years ago, but between his back problems and my (totally irrational) fears of bungee jumping, swimming with sharks, scaling buildings, eating gross insects, and all things smelly—we decided we were better off watching from the couch.

One of the best and worst things about the *Amazing Race*? The flights. At our house, we refer to the legs of the trip that require air travel as "the great equalizer." A team could be blowing through detours and way ahead of the pack, only to get route information directing them to catch the first flight to Hong Kong, which doesn't depart for twelve hours. *Womp womp.* Suddenly, everyone's on the same flight. Any gain is lost.

I wonder if we're not all on the same flight when it comes to sanctification. Sure, you've learned some lessons I haven't yet.

Maybe some of my experiences have yielded growth in areas God hasn't touched in you yet—but if we call ourselves believers, we're not racing to see who we'll beat. Comparing spiritual walks is like comparing our children. They're all different. They develop at different speeds, hit milestones at different times, and then pursue different interests. They're unique and so are our paths to sanctification.

I think about how my children's hobbies have changed as they have gotten older. Gone are the days of "original" artwork. Now they care mostly about *Minecraft* and *Madden*. When they were younger and colored pictures, I'd sometimes hurry them along. "Time to clean up. You're finished, right?" Kaitlyn, the "crafty" one in our family, would always exclaim, "No, I'm still working." Her masterpiece needed more time. I couldn't tell if it was finished or not. I didn't know exactly what she was creating or how elaborate the scene she colored should be. My superficial assessment dismissed the desire and the will of the artist.

Contrast that with my children's current obsession—video games. *Sigh*. It's all levels and attaining points to get to the next stage of play. They know exactly where they are because the game tells them. Quickly, they deduce that level three always follows level two. Their objective becomes discovery and mastery of what's required to reach the next goal rather than the slow work of artistic expression.

Friends, we're all works in progress on the sanctification front. We need to put our controlling tendencies aside and acknowledge that we have no idea what the artist desires to add or erase in us. Likewise, we don't know what he's smoothing or refining in others. From the outside, that woman you compare yourself to may look like a finished product. But you don't know how the Father is changing the landscape of her life.

It's easier to look at life as a video game, isn't it? We picture ourselves on a trajectory, hitting levels as we accumulate points in a system we've derived to measure ourselves. We see the line on the graph headed up and to the right. But that's not the gospel. The gospel doesn't afford us the opportunity to figure out our position as it compares to others. Instead, we must learn to extend grace and fight the tendency to deem ourselves "better" or "worse" than a sister in Christ. We must discipline our eyes and our minds to stay focused on our own lanes of life's track, not worrying over who is ahead of or behind us. Rather, we must encourage each other to finish the race well—no matter the pace (Heb. 12:1–2).

If we could focus on the sanctification journey as the great equalizer, we'd beat down the pride that causes cliques and divides congregations. Comparing levels of spiritual maturity has no healthy outcome. We're all sojourners at varying stages in our sanctification. You have no idea what box of crayons or stickers God is going to pull out to finish others' masterpieces. (Or yours!) We should *all* grow and bear fruit. If you're not, then, friend, let me encourage you: it's time to start.

God is too creative (and compassionate) to use the same approach to complete each of us. How boring would life be if we each had a checklist to accomplish as we graduated our way from level to level? Our comparison dismisses God's gracious artistry. It leaves us watching, waiting, and wondering why our paths are different. But what if it's actually God's sanctifying grace that makes each of our routes unique? It's a blessing that we're not all treated the same. Grace asks us to trade "Am I ahead or behind?" for "I trust you completely."

Takeaway

God's sanctifying grace cures comparison by helping us see our idols, showing us that earthly perfection is not our goal, and reminding us that we're all on individual journeys toward becoming more Christlike. I have no need or reason to compare my journey to anyone else's because God is carefully completing me as an artist finishes a masterpiece.

Comparison-Free Life Action Plan

Read the following passages and write what you observe about sanctifying grace and the work of the Holy Spirit in our lives: Romans 12:3–7, 1 Thessalonians 4:1–8, John 14:17–20, 1 Corinthians 1:30, and 1 Peter 1:1–2.

1. What idols is God working on removing from your life? Review the list of questions provided earlier in this chapter to inform your answer.

2. Would you rather be behind the scenes or in the spotlight? Does the concept of hiding in God's shadow appeal to you? What insufficient shelters (idols like work, food, busyness, or relationships) have you tried to hide in?

3. Have you ever felt like you were ahead of or behind someone in the sanctification process? How did that make you feel about that person? Did it strengthen or harm your relationship?

4. Do you see sanctification as an artist finishing his masterpiece or as a video game? Which concept is more comfortable for you to accept? Did this surprise you?

Memory Verse: "But now that you have been set free from sin and have become slaves of God, the fruit you get leads to sanctification and its end, eternal life" (Rom. 6:22).

Heavenly Father, please help me to recognize your sanctifying work in my life. Help me to run to the safety of your wings instead of the insufficient shelters of idols. And give me more of your grace to stop comparing my journey to the journeys of others. Amen.

Chapter Nine

LIFE IS BIGGER THAN ME

To me, growing into spiritual maturity is becoming less self-conscious and more God-conscious.

–Mark Batterson

I'm a horrible baker, and I've got a Netflix appearance to prove it. It's not that my creations taste bad. *At least not all the time.* It's that they look awful. Sometimes it's difficult to distinguish what they're supposed to be. For instance, a few years ago I served dinner guests banana bread for dessert. *In a bowl.* That's right, I don't like to measure or follow recipes precisely. Who's got time for that? The bread never baked to a proper consistency, so I told them it was banana bread pudding, slapped some whipped cream on top, and handed them spoons.

Of all the things I ever hoped for, being a baking show contestant was the one dream I knew could never come true. We didn't have the Food Network when I was a kid, but I read recipes in magazines and devoured stories about the annual Pillsbury Bake-Off. *Would I ever be bake-off material?* I had a better chance of becoming an NFL linebacker.

Yet God in his infinite care found me the perfect baking show opportunity—a baking show for absolutely terrible bakers. I sent them the photos of my hockey puck cinnamon rolls and the Pinterest lawnmower cake I made my three-year-old. (Picture lime green "grass" with a thick square box of gray fondant in the middle, complete with drinking straw mower handles. Fancy.)

When they told me I made the show, my first thought was, "This is crazy cool grace!" (Okay, my first thought was, "You're kidding me!" and then, "What am I going to wear on TV?" but my third thought was definitely, "Thank you, God, for this grace!") A decade ago, trying to look more "celebrity-like" before heading to LA would have consumed my thoughts. Five minutes after finding out I made the show, I'd have started a new diet and done two hundred crunches. All other priorities would've diminished as I incessantly shopped for outfits. (Between hair, nail, and facial appointments, of course.) Sure, I spent a little time making sure I wouldn't look like a slob, but I didn't obsess over it. (I didn't even get my nails done!)

Since I've already published a book recounting my journey to body image freedom, I'll simply say this: my television experience reminded me of how far I've come. That's what growing grace is all about. After we've received God's saving grace and begun to experience the journey of God's sanctifying grace, it's time to grow. I love how Tim Keller phrases it in many of his sermons: "God sees us as we are, loves us as we are, and accepts us as we are. But by His grace, He does not leave us as we are."[1] The defeat of my body image idol proves the sanctification process in my life, yes! But feeling free to live, pursue dreams, and chase God's purpose for my life, unhindered by body image issues, testifies to growing grace.

God's growing grace enables us to recognize our own skills, talents, and abilities. We can look at the unique ways God has gifted us (and others around us) and then find ways to use them to expand God's kingdom. Growing grace empowers us to live our lives on mission. Like a Marine who's received specific orders, or like a child finishing his broccoli to earn a cookie, we too can laser-beam focus on our purpose so that we don't have to compare ourselves to anyone.

When we experience God's growing grace, we see that life isn't just about us. Rather, we have a job to do. The life of comparison afforded us many opportunities to wonder if *our* job was as important as *her* job or *his* job. But to live comparison-free, we realize that God gave us different talents, and it's our responsibility to use them.

Why Your Talents Matter

In Matthew 25:14–30, Jesus tells a story. It's about a boss who goes on a trip and asks his servants to tend to his property. He gave each one a different amount of talents, based on their ability. One man received five talents, another got two, and a third man just got one.

Okay, let's stop right there for a second. The man didn't give everyone the same amount of talents. One could extrapolate that God didn't give each of us the same amount of talents, either. This may bug you, but sit with that truth for a second, then we'll move on. (Side note: In the story, the word "talent" actually refers to an amount of money—about twenty years' worth of wages. But this parable can easily translate into an important lesson about using our abilities.)

While the big boss was gone, the boys back at the ranch did a little day trading. The guy with five talents bought stock in a booming company and made five more. (Okay, the Bible says he traded, but I picture this guy watching *Mad Money* on CNBC.) The man with two talents used them—he turned that two into four. Doubling your money? Not too shabby. Then there's the guy with one talent. The read-between-the-lines story is that this fellow was not voted "Most Likely to Succeed" in high school. He dug a hole in the ground and hid the master's money.

When the Master returned, he applauded the good investors: "Well done, good and faithful servant. You have been faithful over a little; I will set you over much. Enter into the joy of your master" (Matt. 25:21, 23). But to the guy holding the shovel, he delivered a different message: "You wicked and slothful servant! . . . You ought to have invested my money with the bankers, and at my coming I should have received what was my own with interest" (Matt. 25:26–27). At the end of the chapter, the master condemns the one talent guy to hell! That's serious, folks.

I hate to dampen the mood, but from this illustration, it seems like God cares a *whole* lot about how we use our talents. A member of my "Comparison Crushers" Facebook group posted this:

> Comparison is killing me. Every morning I resolve to do something meaningful with my life, but then I get on social media and within five minutes I'm defeated. There's nothing left to be done. Everything's been tried. And everyone else does it better so why bother? I'm trapped.

I understand her struggle. It seems like every day that I sit down to write this, I see someone else's new book coming out on the same topic.

I wonder if God will take that as an excuse. It's like saying, "Hey, God, I know you gave me this singing talent, but my voice isn't as awesome as Lauren Daigle's, so I sure hope you don't expect me to do anything with it." Should only the best writer write? Should only the most melodious bird sing? If only the best baker baked, it'd sure be difficult to order a birthday cake. We cheat ourselves when we stop using our gifts because we don't feel like we're the best.

What talent has he given you? God's growing grace helps you cultivate and develop it so you can hear those same words that the wise investors heard: "Well done, good and faithful servant."

Growing Your Gifts

Because I don't bake well, I tried to improve before the show. My friend Erin—who used to teach cake-decorating classes—spent an afternoon teaching me how to perfect the texture of buttercream and make icing look like roses. After learning that Crisco is the secret ingredient to good "butter" cream (gross!), I attempted to grow in my baking skills. (Turns out, one lesson wasn't enough! Who knew?)

Most people can quickly list the talents they lack. But do you know what your gifts are? Do you know what skills God gave you to use for his kingdom? Our purposes may not be unique. Someone else may already be doing what we're called to do, but when our stories and personalities collide with our calling, we deliver something that no one else can. That's grace.

Are you an extroverted type with the spiritual gift of teaching? The women's ministry at your church could put you to work. Or maybe you're an introverted planner, administratively gifted. You, my friend, are what every leader needs to get things done. No matter what your assessment, God has a purpose for your life that will not waste any part of how he's made you.

I didn't always believe that. Six months after my first son, Zach, was born, I found myself pregnant again and struggling to keep up with my day job. Though my employer was extremely flexible and I'd cut my hours back significantly, I couldn't handle the stress of work on top of the new mom and pregnancy stress. I cried a lot, freaked out frequently, and—for the sake of my sanity—something had to change. So I quit my job—my well-paying job where I'd spent almost a decade growing in knowledge and leadership.

At the time, I knew God was calling me to focus on being a mom. I presumed God was done using my gifts. Those desires to do TV appearances, write, and speak would be limited to volunteer roles at church—at least for the next eighteen years. *Might as well be forever* . . . I feared.

A scant five years later, I'd just started writing for a new site, the *Dallas Moms Blog*. The co-owner, Lauren, was asked to be on a TV show and wanted no part of it. "Heather, could you do the interview?" she asked. I cried that day. Seriously. I still get choked up thinking about it. How could God have possibly found a way for me to use my communication degree and experience when I wasn't even employed?

God doesn't waste our gifts. Yes, we may have to adjust or put some on hold as we go through certain seasons, but when we're willing, he provides us the opportunity to use our talents.

Melinda (not her real name) is a fifty-two-year-old woman whom I coached through my body image personal training course. For decades, her identity was rooted in her thin and attractive body. But between aging, menopause, and an autoimmune disease, her body changed. She felt lost and wondered if she had anything left to give. I asked Melinda what she liked to do. She didn't know. I asked where she thought she was gifted and what she knew about her personality. She didn't have an answer. She enjoyed cooking and making dinner for others, but she didn't see how using that gift could relieve her struggles with body image and comparison.

I asked Melinda to take some assessments. She had a gift of hospitality—serving and giving to others were the areas she scored highest. I continued to challenge Melinda and asked her to find ways she could use her gifts more regularly. Melinda signed up to deliver meals to people in the church who had babies or deaths in the family. She started paying attention to the needs of those around her, helping when she could. Melinda didn't think her gifts mattered, but now she's a changed person. The more time she spends growing, the more Christ-centered confidence she develops. And she now spends less time stressing over how her body has changed!

Not a Supermodel

A few years ago, God revealed something life-changing to me. I'd recently turned forty, got the last of my babies out of diapers, and written my first book. Ready for this big revelation? *God's purpose for my life did not include modeling.* Shocking, right? I'm barely five-foot-five and shrinking, haven't weighed less than 130 pounds since ninth grade, and am somewhat awkward when placed alone in front of a still camera. On top of all that, launching a supermodel career at my age would be tough.

As ridiculous as this sounds, the concept helped free me. How much of my life had I spent looking at pictures of Cindy Crawford or Elle Macpherson and believing I needed to look more like them to be valuable? How many days did I waste experimenting with new diets or exercise gizmos so I could feel one step closer to beauty? For decades, I pursued changing my appearance with greater vigor than I pursued internal, meaningful growth. I hesitated to pursue my true purpose because I believed I needed to improve the way I looked first.

I love digging into the story of Rachel and Leah with groups of women. Most are shocked when I emphasize something my Sunday school teachers always overlooked: Leah was ugly. Genesis 29:17 uses the conjunction "but" to compare Rachel and Leah. Conjunctions make comparisons. The writer of Genesis could have said "and," but he didn't. God clearly wants us to know that Rachel was hot and Leah was not. To me, this was the meanest verse in the whole Bible. How rude of God to call a woman ugly, right? There's no asterisk in my Bible to explain that Leah had dim eyes but great thighs. We're left with the unsettling juxtaposition of a beautiful girl and her ugly older sister.

Leah's story is harsh in other ways too. Her dad deceptively forces her to marry a man who's got it bad for her sister. Later, she assumes that bearing boys will win her some of his love, but it doesn't work. Yet Leah's story also demonstrates redemption. She has a son named Judah, whose family line, generations later, bears a king named David. Generations after that, Jesus is born from this same branch of Leah's family tree. Leah had great purpose—she's the great (times a bunch) grandmother of the Messiah!

If you knew one of your children or grandchildren would be the next Billy Graham, would that change your purpose in parenting? If I could see how God's purpose for me might impact the future God has planned for my children, I wonder if I'd be as tempted to stare at my phone or watch Netflix instead of reading the Bible together. My purpose isn't just about my growth and me; it's about others too. My ability (or refusal) to use my gifts impacts generations.

In 1 Corinthians 12, speaking about spiritual gifts, Paul encourages the church to remember that they're all part of one body, but each has a different function. In verse 16, Paul illustrates that the ear can't say, "Because I'm not an eye, I do not belong to the body." The ear stays part of the body. Read verses 17 through 19:

> If the whole body were an eye, where would be the sense of hearing? If the whole body were an ear, where would be the sense of smell? But as it is, God arranged the members in the body, each one of them, as he chose. If all were a single member, where would the body be?

If you follow Jesus, you're part of his body, gifted as God chose. I find this amazing. God picked out your gifts! The same one who designed the galaxies and orchestrated nature decided which gifts you, personally, should have. This isn't like your husband trying to pick out an outfit for you. (That doesn't go well in my marriage.) This is he who knows the number of hairs on your head—and everything else about you—picking your gifts. When I think of it this way, it feels foolish to compare my gifts or myself to others.

No matter what you're called to, God has given you everything you need to accomplish his purpose for your life. He'll continue to give you grace to grow in ways that are for his glory and your good.

You're Not Ahead or Behind

Years ago, I took my three-year-old *Cars* fan and two of my babies on a road trip. I'm one of those people who view the GPS arrival time as the "time to beat." I hate wasting time. Why get there at 3:59 when you could arrive at 3:57? I thought my children were too young to notice their mom's driving. That is, until I passed a car and my oldest cried out, "Yay! Mommy wins the race!"

"You got that right, son! Mommy likes winning!" Not just on the highway but in bowling, board games, and debates of all kinds. Oh, and while trying to solve the *Wheel of Fortune* puzzles from the couch. I call them fast and loud.

I'm a tad driven. And sometimes I attempt to get "all the things" done on my own instead of relying on God's grace. But I'm learning that living in God's grace means giving up the race. Success doesn't come from being the first or best. Success comes only through obedience. If God tells you to write, your success comes not from being a best-selling author; it comes from putting words on a page. If God tells you to teach, your success comes not from being teacher of the year, but from instructing faithfully anyone God puts under your influence. Obedience as a singer doesn't mean making a platinum album; it means using your gift every time the opportunity presents itself.

If my strength for living is anything other than 2 Timothy 2:1, "Be strengthened by the grace that is in Christ Jesus," and Hebrews 13:9, "It is good for the heart to be strengthened by grace," I'm going to crash and burn. Chasing success instead of God's will makes it impossible to experience the joy of resting in God's grace.

Growing grace draws me out of scarcity mentality and into a new, grace-filled way of viewing the world. No longer am I in a contest where the one with the "most" or the "best" wins. I'm on my own journey, knowing God will supply all my needs (Phil. 4:19), and that he has a unique purpose for my life that is unaffected by the plan he has for yours (Jer. 29:11).

Inside Out Grace

Paul David Tripp discusses something important to remember during growth—that is, the greatest problem is always inside, not outside, of us. When we convince ourselves that our greatest problems are other people or a lack of something, we deceive ourselves and miss opportunities to experience both sanctification and growth.[2]

Growing grace requires us to venture into untouchable places in our hearts and allow the Holy Spirit to heal them. This healing equips us to carry out Jesus's mission with less drama. The truth is that we don't have any choice but to see the world through the lens of our own experiences. Our individual stories color the way we perceive others and what happens around us. Until we poke at that story and find out what color it tints our world, we'll never be able to grow into the maturity God desires for us. It's like refusing to wear the glasses we need to see the world in focus.

So what's the formula for experiencing God's growing grace in ways that yield life transformation? How do we know when we've arrived? J. I. Packer offers an excellent answer: "We must learn to measure ourselves, not by our knowledge about God, not by our gifts and responsibilities in the church, but by how we pray and what goes on in our hearts. Many of us, I suspect, have no idea how impoverished we are at this level."

A counselor once told me something similar: "Maturity comes when your own sin bothers you more than the sins of others." As you continue to mature in grace, take a look at what you pray for. God's growing grace allows us to live a life of self-forgetfulness, while feeling the supernatural satisfaction that comes from walking in his purpose. In the life of grace, our world becomes bigger than our own needs and wants.

Takeaway

Growing grace cures comparison by showing us that God has a unique purpose for our lives and that he has given us or will give us all that we need to accomplish that purpose. Through God's growing grace, we discover that life isn't about being the best for our own glory; rather, it's about using our talents for his.

Comparison-Free Life Action Plan

Read Matthew 25, 1 Corinthians 12, 2 Timothy 2:1, Hebrews 13:9, Philippians 4:19, and Jeremiah 29:11. What can you glean about God's growing grace and using our talents from these Scriptures?

1. What are you good at? What skills and talents do you believe God has gifted you? What do you know about your personality? (If you've never taken a personality or spiritual gifts assessment, I recommend starting with a SHAPE assessment here: www.freeshapetest.com.)

2. In what ways do you believe that experiencing God's growing grace could affect your proclivity toward comparison?

3. Have you ever been tempted to quit doing something you believed God has called you to do because of comparison? Share with the group or write down a time when resistance and comparison made you stop.

4. What do you find yourself complaining about most? How do you think God feels about this behavior? What can you remind yourself of when you're tempted to complain?

5. Sometimes comparison causes us to lose sight of our dreams and watch the world go by. What God-given dreams do you have for your life? What has stopped you from pursuing these goals? Write about how discovering God's growing grace may empower you to keep trying, learning, and exploring.

Memory Verse: "For we are his workmanship, created in Christ Jesus for good works, which God prepared beforehand, that we should walk in them" (Eph. 2:10).

Heavenly Father, help me to experience your growing grace and to boldly pursue the purpose for which you've created me. Free me from the beast of being "better" and from the pressure to be the best, and instead empower me to serve you faithfully for my good and your glory. Amen.

Chapter Ten

DON'T MISS THE PARTY

Sustaining grace promises not the absence of struggle but the presence of God.

—Max Lucado, *Grace*

Let's talk about suffering.

When my husband started his new job in Austin, I was stuck three hours away waiting for our home to sell. No one came to see it during the six weeks it was on the market, though I had to reshine floors and counters every time I dared to leave. Just in case. It was hard to be solo. (Major props to all single mothers, military spouses, and wives of men who travel a ton. You're amazing!) I stunk at this.

He'd been gone ten days and challenges abounded. First, there was the morning I startled awake at four A.M. because I saw bright lights and heard a man shouting in Spanish. Frightened, but knowing I was the only one there to save the children, I determinedly sprang out of bed to investigate. As I slowly pushed open my bedroom door, I discovered the noise and light were coming from the television. Apparently, it had come on by itself and, somehow, found a channel with a Mexican clown doing a monologue. The clown freaked me out, as did the fact that we don't have cable. Even if our "smart" TV had turned itself on, there are no Spanish channel apps. I'm still trying to solve this mystery.

Then, the next night, I got everyone in bed early. I felt excited about the prospect of free time to sit in bed and read. At 9:15 P.M., I heard a chirp. Then another. And another. The kids began to yell from their beds, "Mom, what's that noise?" *Argh!* The smoke detector. After scouring the kids' toys for AA batteries, I fixed the chirping one. I thought we could call it a night. Back in bed, ten minutes later, another chirp. The smoke detector in the next room decided to join the party. This one taunted from the high ceiling of my oldest son's room. He and I carried the seven-foot ladder from the garage up the stairs so I could yank it from the ceiling and make the beeping stop. Problem solved. To bed again. Thirty minutes later, I'm groggy and half asleep, and wouldn't you know it. More beeping, this time from my youngest boys' bedroom! I move the ladder and, with my son holding his bedside reading light, pull it off the ceiling.

I was so tired. I wanted that house sold so we could all live in the same city and so my husband could take care of middle-of-the-night encounters with creepy clowns and smoke detectors. I recognize my suffering—even in this scenario—rates so light it's comical. I hesitate even to approach the topic of suffering because God has been very gracious to me in this area. Though I've suffered through the loss of loved ones, relational struggles, and minor health trials, I've experienced nothing like those who have battled cancer, lost a child, or been martyred for their faith. I'd sit with you through these trials, but I'd have nothing to say.

My suffering is akin to getting a pedicure and complaining that the lady pressed the sloughing brush too aggressively against my delicate heels. I tread lightly.

You may have suffered much. Or you may think my pedicure example sounds pretty trying. But here's the truth about sustaining grace: it's good for each of life's trials. No matter what we endure, his grace promises to be enough.

Don't Help the Baby Sea Turtles

My parents' condo is on Florida's Space Coast, and it's a huge breeding ground for sea turtles. Many summers, we've watched these size-of-my-palm mini creatures emerge from the sea grass and embark on an often-dangerous journey toward the ocean. This trek is a rite of passage for the turtles. When they're ready, they leave without directions or a parent to lead them. They trust their instincts to head toward the light coming from the open horizon. They don't have the Waze app telling them where to turn.

One evening we were on the beach, and we witnessed two little turtles on their trek. One turtle, likely the older sibling, darted toward his destination and disappeared into the surf. The other seemed confused. He rushed toward the crashing waves, then turned back. He ran parallel to the water, only to do a full turn the other way. Only one in one thousand sea turtles will make it to adulthood. This guy's future was iffy.

I wanted to help him—to pick him up and carry him to the waves before a crab or giant seagull ate him for dinner! To stand by and watch him struggle was painful. But I knew from the signs posted everywhere that you should never help a hatchling. Don't touch them; stay out of their way. Not allowing them to struggle heightens their risk of death when they face their first obstacles in the water. Eventually, the tiny turtle inched his way into the surf.

His journey wasn't as quick or as easy as his brother's. But there's a good chance, because we were standing nearby, he stayed safe from flying predators. Had he been alone, he may have faced a different fate.

As I think about God's sustaining grace, I'm forced to examine what I really believe about suffering. Growing up, I heard messages like "Life is what *you* make it!" Culturally, this tone was popular. They didn't want kids like me to think about how hard life was because then we'd be discouraged and never "Shoot for the stars!" I remember seeing adults face difficult circumstances. But somehow, I chose to ignore the truth and adopt the vain belief that if I worked hard enough and made the "right" decisions, I could avoid struggle.

A Disney-tinted view of life made it difficult to accept anything hard that came my way. At twenty-five, I faced a crisis of faith after running a U.S. Congressional race. My candidate lost narrowly after his opponent smeared him in a last-minute barrage of twisted words. It didn't seem fair. We were the good guys; they were the bad. What kind of economy does God run where he blesses the cheaters? I wondered and I doubted him.

My pastor recently explained how reality is always more empowering than lies. If we accept that struggle is a normal part of life, then we can face and even expect difficulty. We aren't ruined when life reaps pain. But if we view suffering as injustice—as a variance from the way things are "supposed to be"—then we'll feel devastated and let down when life isn't full of good hair days and free lattes. This discouragement opens the window for comparison's henchmen (envy and covetousness) to make us even more miserable.

The first thing to remember about God's sustaining grace is that God is with us in every struggle. He doesn't leave us to fend for ourselves, to try and find the beach on our own. No, he's there, walking beside us as we learn endurance, patience, and where to place our hope. One verse that comes to mind is 2 Corinthians 12:9: "My grace is sufficient for you." How many times in your life have you felt lack and been reminded of this? If this isn't your go-to when the enemy reminds you of what you're missing, fight FOMO (fear of missing out) by memorizing this Scripture.

Does God Still Love You?

God's sustaining grace embraces us every time the enemy taunts us with this lie: "God no longer loves you. If he did, you wouldn't be suffering." There's a good chance comparison has chimed in here too. "It's *not* fair. You're the only one who's struggling. *She* has it so good. *She's* never faced this problem. I wonder why God isn't good to you?" Have you heard that one? I sure have.

We planted a church several years ago. Neither my husband nor I expected it to be as challenging as it was. I cried over that church hundreds of times. We did the things and prayed the prayers, yet growth happened at sloth speed. I stood in the foyer of our elementary school location, praying God would send people. A car turned in, and I'd fill with anticipation. Smile plastered on my face, I'd head toward the door to greet the newcomer, only to watch the car pull out again. They didn't need a church—just a place to turn around.

Every year (sometimes multiple times a year), we decided to quit. We asked God questions that started with what, why, and when. Yet for seven full years, God sustained us to continue. I wish I could tell you that God gave us a heaping dose of grace that first year—and we rode that high through year seven. I begged him many times to give me a glimpse of the future so I'd have the strength to endure. *Just show me it'll all be okay, someday, God! Please?* But he never did. He only gave us the strength to carry on one day at a time.

If you're in the midst of suffering, let me also encourage you to remember this truth. God's grace is sufficient, but it's not a one and done prayer. His mercies are new every morning (Lam. 3:22–23). Every day we must ask for a fresh dose of that grace. There are parts of the future I wish God had revealed to me ahead to give me hope. But had I fully glimpsed what was coming, there were other parts I could not have endured. It's grace that we can't see the future.

How does God's sustaining grace rescue us from the life of comparison? There are three key ways a deeper understanding of God's sustaining grace helps us live comparison-free:

- It reminds us of God's sovereignty.
- It grows our ability to extend grace to others.
- It reminds us we have a hope that cannot be crushed.

God's Sovereignty

Sometimes it's hard to see God's sovereign hand, especially in the face of suffering.

Tim Keller offers the most reasonable explanation I've ever read as to how we can reconcile the truth of God's goodness and love for us with the reality that terrible things happen in this world. Keller argues that if God is powerful and infinite enough to take the heat for "allowing" evil, then he must also be powerful and infinite enough to have good reasons for it.[1] Understanding God's sovereignty is key to experiencing the freedom found in the life of grace.

- If God is sovereign, he is in control. Complete control. I don't need to be.
- If God is sovereign, he already knows my future. I don't have to stress, try to manipulate outcomes, or despair. He's got it, even when it doesn't look like it's all coming together the way it "needs" to.

- If God is sovereign, I can stop believing that I know what's best for me and rest in the truth that only he does. This means trusting that I have all I need.

I'm not saying it's easy to affirm God's sovereignty. It takes faith, trust, and grace. Sustaining grace. I love how J. I. Packer says, "You don't get awe until you cultivate the sense that God is very great and you are very small."

We need more awe. The almighty God, creator of the universe, is exceedingly more qualified in life design than you or me. Life will always go better when we surrender our master plan and submit to the Master's plan. When I look at it through eyes of grace, I'm glad I'm not in charge.

Grace for Others

Sharing is hard. Isn't it? We pretend it's not, of course. *Share! Share! Share!* I yelled it like an expletive thousands of times during my first few years of parenting. I mean, we do share. Yawns and bad moods effortlessly convey between us. But when it comes to what's mine: my time, my money, my toys—deep down, I'd rather you get your own.

Sharing grace feels hard until we've discovered that we have all we need. Comparison further divides us. I don't want to give you grace; I covet what you have. I don't want to see you do better—at least not while I'm still struggling. Envy magnifies the differences in our plots. If I treat you generously, you may get further ahead! If I share with you from what's mine, what if you take it and leave me in the dust?

As you read this, you may think about sharing resources—money, even. But sometimes it can be as simple as refusing to share a kind word.

Before our move, I sat in the lobby of yet another hotel. We were visiting my husband in Austin, and he'd already headed to work. I put on cropped black workout pants, the tank top I'd worn the day before, and a dressy black cardigan sweater. Why the dressy sweater, you ask? Because the lobby featured subzero temperatures, and it was the only thing in my suitcase with sleeves! I skipped the makeup, and my unwashed hair was in a ponytail. (Don't picture a cute, coiffed pony. No, this one was a mess, as if I couldn't find the brush. Because, technically, I couldn't.) But the kids were hungry. So I filled plates with Texas-shaped waffles, bacon, and enough fruit to feed a small nation. Finally, with children settled, I grabbed myself a cup of coffee and took a deep breath. Then she walked in.

Her stunning green dress caught my eye. I loved the sleeves, and her shoes matched perfectly. Her long, curly hair and well-applied makeup showed me she had somewhere important to be this morning. She dropped a load of business books on the table before she filled her plate. I realized I'd been staring at her for at least a minute. She caught my eye, and I smiled awkwardly. I took a few more sips of coffee and then felt prompted to compliment her. *Compliment, her? Yeah, God. Right? Don't you think I'm the one who needs the encouragement today? Not Miss Perfect Green Dress?*

I'm learning to be more obedient in these situations. A child needed a napkin, so as I walked by her table, I said, "That's a gorgeous dress." I don't think I slowed down during the delivery, but I said it. *Happy, God?* As I returned to the table with the napkins, she looked at me and softly replied, "You don't know how much I needed that today." I stuttered over a few more compliments. "What? You look great. Whatever you've got planned, you look great. Really great."

Then I almost started to cry as I was reminded of a truth I know but often forget. The woman who looks like she has it all together often feels like she's falling apart. I know because I used to be that woman. A decade ago, I would have had a very difficult time saying anything to her. I would've felt too self-conscious over my own appearance to approach the throne of someone who was better dressed. Plus, I would have been so busy comparing myself to her that I may not have wanted to compliment her at all. That would be an acknowledgment of the truth that she was ahead in the imaginary "who looks prettiest" contest.

Every person you know desperately needs grace. Women who cross your path in hotel lobbies need grace. Women who look and act like they've got it all together need grace. Women who look like they're falling apart need grace. Your husband needs grace. Your children need grace. Your parents need grace. Your friends need grace. Your weird neighbor and that annoying lady who always illegally parks her Escalade in the fire lane for preschool pickup? Yes, they need grace too. Everyone on the planet needs grace. Make sure you have enough so you can share.

When you receive and acknowledge the miracle of God's grace, you're able to act as an agent of this grace. You're free to encourage others without feeling that their success may mean your failure. (Remember that abundance mentality?) The degree to which we've received and internalized this grace is the degree to which we'll be able to extend it to others.[2]

Can I tell you something bizarre that happened to me a few days after the hotel incident? I was in Target picking up an order after cleaning for another "maybe this will be the day" house showing. I know my hair looked like I just got done with a shift in a sweatshop. Yet a stunning woman, twenty years younger than me, handed me my package and said, "Wow. You are so beautiful." Though years ago I would have recommended she find a good optometrist, that day I smiled and thanked her. Truth is, I needed some encouragement. Her words were a gift. Hmm . . . I wonder if when we overflow with grace, God allows even more to splash our way.

Hope That Cannot Be Crushed

Jesus told a story about a man with two sons. The younger one took his inheritance and squandered it on cheap thrills. The older one stayed home, continued to work for his father, and never acted the fool. (At least, not in the same way his brother did.) Eventually, the little brother went broke. Starving and penniless, he returned home, told his father he was sorry, and begged to be a servant in his household again. The father greeted him with compassion and, instead of making the son pay for his foibles, rejoiced that he was home. He threw a party.

So, perhaps you've heard the story of the prodigal son before. Whether you relate more to the older brother or the younger, here's what I hope you'll see in the parable from Luke 15. The older brother misses the party. He's envious, maybe jealous too. "I've served you faithfully, and you don't even buy the pizza when my friends come over. But now this fool is back and you're serving filet mignon? How is this fair?" (My paraphrase, of course.)

When we act like the older brother, saying to God, "Why'd you let her get this?" or "How is it fair that she's pregnant and I'm not?," we miss the party. Sustaining grace reminds us that God is always there. All that our Father has is ours. When we dwell in the richness of God's grace, we're better able to extend that grace to others. When we feel tempted to compare, we should meditate on the ways we've experienced God's grace personally and rejoice in all that we already have through him.

Without grace, we miss the party. And, goodness, how I hate to miss a good party.

The temptation to miss the party and wallow in my "struggle" is very real for me. Like when we moved, I remember feeling homeless. We'd said our goodbyes and attended farewell parties. Eric started his new job, and weekends were spent traveling to Austin and trying to assimilate into our new church's culture. But we lingered "in between" for months. How I longed to be settled somewhere. We had no new address, yet I couldn't relax in the home we were selling. There's no leaving clothes on top of the dryer or dishes in the sink when you're in "show" mode. I felt like I couldn't fully live in either place.

Isn't this the same tension we face as believers? We struggle because earth isn't our home. We may feel plagued with the dissatisfaction that comes from knowing we'll never be at total peace until we're in eternity with Jesus. Certain issues—the temptation to compare, even—will taunt our hearts until heaven. Fortunately, God understands the conflict and offers his sustaining grace until we make the transition. We only need to rely on it. I love to read Psalm 54:4 in tough times: "Behold, God is my helper and ally; The Lord is the sustainer of my soul [my upholder]" (AMP). But my favorite verse that can become our prayer when we really need God's sustaining grace is Psalm 119:116: "LORD, sustain me as you promised, that I may live! Do not let my hope be crushed" (NLT).

What kind of hope can't be crushed? There's only one kind, really. That's hope in Jesus. 1 Peter 1:13 exhorts us to be sober-minded and to "*set your hope fully on the grace* that will be brought to you at the revelation of Jesus Christ" (emphasis mine). Friend, your hope is not in a better life. Put that burden down. Neither is your hope found at the end of your struggle. Even if you're in the middle of a hard season, hope is insufficient if its only goal is to see the long winter end. Our true hope is not that the sun will shine again, but that the Son never stopped lighting our way. His grace alone must be where our hope finds anchor. Anywhere else we place it has the potential to disappoint us. But if our hope is found in Christ alone, comparison can't con us into believing God has forgotten.

Takeaway

Sustaining grace cures comparison with the truth that even in times of struggle, God is sovereignly in control. When we live in his grace, we can share his grace and not "miss the party" by falling for comparison's lies. Our ultimate hope is not just that something better lies on the other side of our struggle; it's in Jesus.

Comparison-Free Life Action Plan

Read through Psalm 54:4, Psalm 119:6, Psalm 68:20, Psalm 140:7, and 1 Peter 1:13. What do these verses teach about God's sovereignty and his sustaining grace? What is God's role when we face struggle?

1. How does knowing God is with us, even when our circumstances feel bleak, help us not to compare ourselves to others?

2. Have you ever heard the lie that if God loved you more, you wouldn't be suffering so much? Can you share or think of a time when you were suffering and wondered, "Why me?"

3. Does it bring you comfort to know that God is sovereign? Is it hard or easy for you to accept this truth and submit your "master plan" to the Master's plan?

4. What situations in life cause you to focus on what you lack or to "miss the party"?

Memory Verse: "But he said to me, 'My grace is sufficient for you, for my power is made perfect in weakness.' Therefore I will boast all the more gladly of my weaknesses, so that the power of Christ may rest upon me" (2 Cor.12:9).

Heavenly Father, please help me in my suffering—both great and small. Help me to remember your sovereign plan and trust you when I can't see the way. Help me to not "miss the party" in comparing my sufferings to those of the people around me. Instead, free me to rest in your grace. Amen.

Section Three

A LIFE OF GRATITUDE

Chapter Eleven

DISCOVER CONTENTMENT

Contentment makes poor men rich;
discontent makes rich men poor.
–Benjamin Franklin

The day before my wedding, one task ranked more important than many of the others: my spray tan appointment.

I'd tried spray tanning a few times before, just to make sure I liked the look. But a spray tan booth expert I was not. The start of the spray startled me. Every time. This knocked me out of the proper tanning position. Every time. I'd scramble to recover—holding my arms away from my body (who wants stark white armpits?) and closing my eyes without scrunching my face (tiger stripes are not my look). But, sadly, no one reminded me to keep my head up. My fake tan intensified overnight and, by the morning of my wedding, a football-shaped white spot extended from the bottom of my chin to the base of my neck. It was not pretty. Trust me. To cover it, I wore foundation from the tip of my forehead, down my neck, all the way to the top of my dress. My apologies to everyone I hugged that day. I sure hope the Beige 4 stain came out. *Sorry.*

I fail to keep my head up in other places too—beyond just tanning beds. Too often, I walk with my head down. I'm watching for obstacles on the path, I suppose. In my twenties, I used to jog the same way, until a friend coached me with some truth: "You run faster when you're looking forward. Don't look down. Don't look beside you. Just look straight ahead, to the horizon."

Isn't that true for our lives too? Comparison keeps us looking around to see how we're pacing others. Envy, covetousness, and pride keep us looking down—scrutinizing the sidewalk, wishing for life to be different. But the life of grace should be a life of deeply rooted gratitude in which we can lay down the burden of comparison and refocus our drive and ambition into finding God's best. It's impossible to live comparison-free, unless you are grace-filled. I hope that exploring God's saving grace, sanctifying grace, growing grace, and his sustaining grace has helped you gain a deeper understanding of how God's grace touches every part of our lives.

In the absence of God's great grace, any other avenue toward "not caring what others think" or "being comfortable in your own skin" is just pride in disguise. Similarly, unless you replace your comparison habit with other, healthier habits comparison will creep back in.

Once during an interview, I was asked this question: "What's the first thing someone should do if they want to stop comparing?" After talking about idolatry and grace for a few seconds, I gave her the same answer the Apostle Paul gives throughout his letters: find contentment.

Does that word make you bristle? Contentment can sound elusive. In 1 Timothy 6, Paul tells the younger Timothy to fill his life with "great gain" through godliness and contentment. In verse 7, he reminds all who thirst for more material possessions, status, or money of a truth you've likely heard before: "We brought nothing into the world, and we cannot take anything out of the world." He continues, "But if we have food and clothing, with these we will be content." A pantry full of food and a closet full of clothing are enough for contentment? *Wow! Life must have been simpler back then!*

Friend, I won't pretend that contentment in our culture comes easy. We must choose to see the world through lenses of grace. Practically, this means adding a gratitude filter to our view of life. Every morning, we must wake up and make a choice. Will I look for evidence of God's grace to be thankful for, or will I let pride, envy, covetousness, and complaining tint my existence? Will I keep searching for greener grass or decide to water my own lawn? Will I look down and around, bemoaning what *could* or *should* have been, or will I hold my head high and run the race Christ has set before me?

Cut Out Complaining

I hate to admit it, but sometimes I complain about my life. Discontentment takes root and grows leaves. I spend too much time "wishing" things were different. And by different, I mean the way *I* think it should go. Everyone should act like they're *supposed* to (and think like me, of course).

Yikes. My pride. I'm thankful God's sanctifying grace is still at work. I'm also thankful that he deals with me (at least so far) more gently than he dealt with the Israelites. If you're looking for biblical examples of why we should learn to be content, read the book of Numbers. In Numbers 11, the Israelites, who experienced some incredible demonstrations of God's faithfulness (they walked through the parted Red Sea, for Pete's sake!), complain about their situation in the desert.

God became so angered by their complaining that he set fire to their camp. Moses had to call a prayer meeting and beg God to tame the flames. But the fire wasn't enough to snuff the complaining from their hearts. Instead, the Israelites continued grumbling. What could possibly be so important as to cause the complainers to ignore God's warning? Meat.

Okay, now, as someone with type B blood, I often have a strong craving for beef. A few days without meat and my brain function diminishes. I feel ravenous enough to chew on my fingers. My doctor once put me on a vegan diet for twenty-one days. Blood work done afterward revealed that everything in my body went wacky. As she reviewed the test results, she said something like, "Hmm . . . I think you're one of those people who can't go without meat." I didn't really hear what she said because I was fantasizing about hamburgers.

I doubt this was the case for the Israelites. What I see in Scripture is how God provided everything they needed for nourishment in their morning manna. I doubt they could blame their complaining on vegan diet–induced hormonal imbalances. God speaks through Moses, saying, "Therefore the Lord will give you meat, and you shall eat. You shall not eat just one day, or two days, or five days, or ten days, or twenty days, but a whole month, until it comes out at your nostrils and becomes loathsome to you, because you have rejected the Lord who is among you" (Num. 11:18–20).

God's like, "You want meat? I'll give you meat. I'll give you so much meat that you'll never ask me for meat again." It's a conversation I've had with my children once or twice. "You're bored? Okay, I'll help you not be bored. In fact, after we sell all your toys, I can come up with a whole list of chores so that you'll never be bored again!" (More evidence that we're made in his image, right?)

Then the story gets interesting. Instead of Moses just relaying God's message, he gets caught up in logistics. Moses asks God, "Uh,

Lord, there are like six hundred thousand people down here. How are you going to give us a month's worth of meat for this many mouths?" God isn't fond of this question and says to Moses, "Is the LORD's hand shortened? Now you shall see whether my word will come true for you or not" (Num. 11:23).

Next, God sends massive amounts of quail. The complainers stuff themselves with meat for a little while and then, boom! God strikes them dead with a plague! *Yikes!* The Bible says the meat was still in their teeth as he knocked them off, and "there they buried the people who had the craving" (Num. 11:34). So God wiped out a bunch of people because they wanted meat and complained about it?

I'm glad God extends copious amounts of grace to me. Oh, the times he surely heard me complain about unmet pregnancy cravings—or the time I threw a fit to my husband because the bottled water he'd brought me from the convenience store wasn't cold enough. *Sigh.* We're receiving grace even when we don't acknowledge it. But living in discontentment is destructive and distracting. God wants more for us.

Contentment versus Complaining

Our first step on the road to contentment is to stop complaining. In 1 Corinthians 10:6, Paul tells us that these things happened to the Israelites as examples for us. Though God may not pummel me to death with cold water bottles when I gripe over tepid Dasani, we're accountable to know better.

I hate it when my children complain. One whines, "We don't have the granola bars I like. Why don't you ever buy the kind I like, Mom?" After explaining that I only buy what's on sale, I feel frustrated that I have to justify myself to an eight-year-old. There are a *lot* of other options in the pantry. Kids in third-world countries don't get their choice of granola bars. Be grateful and eat chips.

(Illustration purposes only. I'd never encourage my children to eat chips. I meant to write organic apples there. *Sure.*)

Does God hear my complaints in the same way? The book of Numbers implies that he does. Why don't I have a body like *hers*? Why don't I have a house like *hers?* Why can't my children act more like *hers*? Why can't I go on a vacation like *that*? The list of things I feel justified to complain about could fill a page. One meme on Pinterest put it all in perspective brilliantly. Marine Staff Sergeant Johnny Joey Jones lost both his legs when a bomb exploded while he was serving in Afghanistan. The image showed Johnny, standing on two prosthetic legs. But it's the quote written over the photo that convicted me. It read: "People ask how I can stay so positive after losing my legs. . . . I simply ask how they can stay so negative with theirs."

The more I experience every aspect of God's grace, the more I realize that complaining is clearly sin. Complaining insinuates we know better than God does what's best for us. It reinforces the idolatry of our hearts and deceives us into believing we'd be more content if we got everything we put on our dream boards.

Understand I'm not talking about lament. We lament when we grieve our circumstances while still surrendered to the sovereignty of God. I've prayed those prayers. Maybe you have too, recently even. "God, this is so hard. Please fix it. Take it away. Change my circumstances, please!" The difference? The lamenting heart begs God from a heart of gratitude, while the complaining heart shouts at God as if he hasn't done enough.

Even Psalmists Struggled with Contentment

In Psalm 73, Asaph, the author of this passage, confesses that his "feet had almost slipped." How did he almost stumble away from the one true God? One word. Envy (Ps. 73:3).

Asaph wasn't a "nobody" in Old Testament times. He was a prominent Levite. He was a famous singer and songwriter, in charge of all of the music for King David. He also served as a "seer" (or prophet) in the courts of the king. Consider him a combination of royal counselor and Chris Tomlin. He had social standing. He lived a comfortable life.

But Asaph outlived both kings he served, David and Solomon. He watched Jerusalem crumble as the kingdom was torn into north and south. The temple was in ruins. The people suffered while their wicked leaders built idols and abandoned the Lord (1 Kings 11–14; 2 Chron. 11–12). Times were tough, and as Asaph's discomfort grew, so did his envy of the arrogant and the wicked. It's as if Asaph had Instagram. First, he envies their "healthy and strong" bodies (Ps. 73:4). Then, in verse 12, he idolizes their "carefree" lives. It's like Asaph's scrolling through their workout videos and vacation photos while he's trapped in his room at the retirement home.

Asaph wonders if his years of following God have all been in vain. Though he's tried to do things the Lord's way, he questions if it's made any difference at all. Asaph suffers while the wicked succeed. How can this be fair? Perhaps you can relate?

Then, something fascinating happens. As if snapping himself out of a dream—abruptly halting his own spiraling thoughts—Asaph turns his heart to worship. In verses 16 and 17, Asaph confesses that he couldn't make sense of it all until he went "into the sanctuary of God." Then, he remembered that this life is not the end game—it's neither the parade nor our home, to reference our earlier discussions. The wicked may seem to prosper now, but that won't always be their fate. He then pens poetic words to remind his own heart of God's faithfulness. Look at Psalm 73:23–26:

> Nevertheless, I am continually with you;
>   you hold my right hand.

You guide me with your counsel,
and afterward you will receive me to glory.
Whom have I in heaven but you?
And there is nothing on earth that I desire besides you.
My flesh and my heart may fail,
but God is the strength of my heart and my portion forever.

The second step on the way to finding contentment is to turn your heart to worship. The temptation to compare ourselves to others, to envy, to covet—they may never go away. But, you can choose how you respond when each temptation comes. We can choose to follow Asaph's example and turn our hearts to worship.

Start by thanking God that our debt is paid and our future is secure—no matter what else happens. We can remember to thank God for supplying all of our needs, "according to his riches in glory in Christ Jesus" (Phil. 4:19). And we can worship him in majesty—an act that reemphasizes to our spirits the greatness of God and his immeasurable power and worth.

If you find yourself in an "envy spiral" like Asaph and need help turning your heart to worship, read the Psalms or put on some God-focused worship music and sing along. Cultivating a heart of worship will help you grow in contentment.

It's Not About Me

There's one big reason worship is so effective at stifling comparison and growing us in contentment. That is surrender. Worship re-emphasizes the truth that life isn't only about us. I think of 2 Corinthians 5:15: "And he died for all, that those who live *might no longer live for themselves* but for him who for their sake died and was raised" (emphasis mine). Isn't that why we get caught in the life of comparison, anyway? Our perspective becomes too narrow, too self-focused. Instead of seeing ourselves as microscopic organisms in the vastness of God's universe, we discreetly decide we're the sun. Everything should revolve around us.

It's fascinating to consider what happened to our nation—and our world—during the COVID-19 pandemic. For a period in time, most of us stopped thinking about our agendas and gladly quarantined to serve the greater good. We laid down our vacation plans, extracurricular activities, and "lives as normal" in submission to the government's plea to think of others first. Sure we had some squabbles over toilet paper and canned veggies, but collectively we demonstrated that we can view our lives as a tiny pixel in the scheme of the world's screen.

Outside of times of crisis, it's harder to keep that mentality. More often than I care to admit, I worry about me first. And when I grumble, complain, fuss, and beg for my own way, I imply that I know what's best for me. I demand (often passive-aggressively) that someone (God) fulfill my wishes, or else. (Watch out! I'm really good at giving the silent treatment.) I picture the bratty little Veruca Salt character from the classic movie *Charlie and the Chocolate Factory,* walking around the facility and demanding to have everything she touches, singing, "Don't care how . . . I want it now!" Like a mini-terrorist, she threatens to scream if Daddy doesn't deliver.

I'd never expose you to a musical number recounting all the ways my life *could* be better if God would just do what *I* want him to do in my life, but let me assure you, there are days my heart hums a similarly self-centered tune. That's when I need to worship. Worship jolts me back to the truth that there is only one who is worthy. And it's not me!

It's Not Hiding

The *Online Etymology Dictionary* explains that the word contentment derives from the mid-fifteenth century word (also contentment), which meant "satisfactory payment" of a debt. Could it be that finding contentment is as simple as understanding that our debt is paid? The word contentment is passive, implying you don't have to *do* anything to get contentment. You only have to receive it. The pressure is off. We pursue happiness, search for satisfaction, and stalk better, but we don't have to chase contentment—we need only rest in it. Contentment isn't hiding. Contentment is found when we deepen our understanding of grace.

Here's another way to think about it. Contentment and grace are BFFs—best friends forever. Once you've embraced grace, you discover that contentment has always been there, right beside it, smiling and wearing the other half of the heart-shaped "Be Fri" necklace. This dynamic duo of grace and contentment is just waiting for you to say, "Come on in."

It's impossible to be content without grace. Why? Because grace allows us to recognize, once and for all, that life's not fair. You know those little lawyers inside our heads who argue that we deserve more than we have? They rest their case when they see just how beautifully unfair grace is. In the comparison-free, grace-filled life, contentment becomes a tangible reality. So how do we actually live this way? That's where gratitude comes in.

Gratuitous Gratitude

My son Zach studies Latin, and we both find it fun to try to figure out what words mean based on their roots. The word *gratuitus* stumped me. It sounded like gratitude, which I define as thankfulness. But it also sounded like gratuitous, which means "uncalled for" or "unjustified," as in *gratuitous violence*. Which is the more accurate definition?

Turns out, *gratuitus* is best defined as given freely or spontaneous. Our word gratitude derives from a similar Latin word *gratia,* which means pleasing or thankful. Guess what this word also means? It means grace. In other words, the life of grace *is* the life of *gratuitus* gratitude.

The third step on the road to contentment, after cutting out complaining and turning your heart toward worship, is to cultivate a heart of gratitude. When grace-soaked gratitude swells, comparison shrinks. Zooming the camera lens to take a micro look at God's grace in our lives lets us see it all the more clearly. Gratuitous gratitude is free and spontaneous thankfulness, always. There are more than forty-two verses in the Bible about giving thanks, many of them instructional. Hebrews tells us to continually offer God a sacrifice of praise (Heb. 13:15), while the psalmist talks about praise and thanksgiving dozens of times. Paul tells us in Philippians 4:6–7 that gratitude is part of the equation to cure anxiety. We need gratitude to burst from our beings—so much so that outside observers deem us odd!

Science is catching up to the Bible's recommendations for living. God created our bodies *and* our minds, so it only makes sense that he'd know what to do to keep them healthy. While complaining can stress our brains, practicing gratitude helps you stay sane. Researchers at UC Davis found that people who work daily to have an attitude of gratitude reduced their amounts of the stress hormone cortisol by 23 percent. With stress hormones under control, they also experienced improved mood and energy levels and less anxiety![1]

Those stains that comparison leaves—the ones we discussed in Section One of this book—can literally be wiped away with gratitude. Researchers found that keeping a gratitude journal actually increases the amount of activity in the hypothalamus part of your brain. This increased activity leads to less anxiety, better sleep, and fewer aches and pains, and it may even cause you to exercise more. In other words—spend fifteen minutes writing down your blessings each morning, and you may actually *want* to go to the gym! I've never seen a gratitude journal recommended on any diet plan.

Gratitude also has the power to reshape neural pathways and give you a burst of dopamine—the happy chemical produced in your brain that makes you feel less depressed, more energetic and motivated, and even more content. Guess what? That dopamine helps you fend off cravings and addictions while helping you feel focused, happier, and healthier.[2]

You don't have to become the "ideal you" to stop comparing and start living. Instead, practice gratitude, and you may start to feel like the life you live is already pretty great!

Blessings Are Everywhere

My seven-year-old, Drew, loves sloths. He's the slowest eater in our family, and we sometimes refer to him as Tail-End Charlie because he's usually lagging a few steps behind everyone else. I'm not sure when his obsession with sloths began, but we decided to turn this into a learning opportunity. Through research, we discovered that sloths sleep fifteen hours a day and only come down from their canopy once a week to clear their bowels.

Imagine our surprise when we visited the sloth habitat at the San Diego Zoo and arrived just as this fascinating creature climbed down. The statistical odds of us being there at that exact moment—when we could see the sloth eye-level from a few feet away—were extremely low. After shooting a zillion photos, I stood amazed. How did that happen? How did *we* plan that so perfectly? My husband's response was, "That's not us. That's grace." He says it a lot, actually. And now I'm getting better at seeing it too. I knew better than to use the word luck, right? (Christians aren't lucky; we're blessed. Or so I heard all through childhood each time I said, "They're so lucky.") Sloth sightings are grace-filled blessings.

A few days later, we went on a boat ride. The captain told us we might see some whales but made no guarantee. It was the right time of year, but he hadn't spotted any during his last few trips. An hour into the ride, the most amazing thing happened. We saw a huge, gray back surface from the water only to flip back in again. Then we saw another. And another. A whale-watching boat with tracking technology passed us, and we followed them. This led to a full afternoon of awe, wonder, and me repeating, "Look! There's another one!"

When we see life through the filter of grace, it brims with God's blessings, both whale-sized and barely visible. You can write it off as "being in the right place at the right time," but then you miss the chance of appreciating every opportunity as a gift from your good father. You miss the chance to express gratitude.

Want to find more contentment? Look for little blessings everywhere. Track them mentally and write them down. Actively look for his gifts, and you'll soon learn to rest in contentment. Like sloths and whales, we'll find them if we're watching. Free office lunches. Being the ninth caller to win. Empty parking spaces near the door. Utility bill refunds. Sunshine on your last day of vacation. They're all evidence of grace.

Why Not Be Grateful?

My friend Melissa and I tried to get on *The Price Is Right* once. I still have my yellow price tag sticker that reads "Heather" in giant print. Though they never called me to "come on down," I'm still a fan. I love game shows. The chance to spin a wheel and score a trip to the Bahamas? Sounds fun. I'm in!

Have you ever watched a game show where the contestant's response seemed somewhat out of line with what he or she won? Last week, the kids and I watched a show where the contestant could have won a hundred thousand dollars! All he needed to do was identify some celebrities by name. But the poor fellow couldn't name one. His winnings? Just one thousand dollars—a consolation prize. His response? He exuberantly shouted "Yes!" and jumped with praise hands held high, as if he'd won a million! The show's host seemed concerned that the man didn't realize how little he was taking home.

Friend, each and every day we have a choice. We can win a thousand dollars and see only the ninety-nine thousand we didn't get, then feel let down, disappointed, or worse as we listen to comparison tell us we're losers who missed out—big time. Or we can be like the enthusiastic game show contestant. The truth is, he left the show a thousand dollars richer than he came. Why not be grateful? Why not be excited? Why not see the glass half-full?

When our hearts are grateful, we give them permission to be enthusiastic. The word *enthusiasm* is derived from the Latin roots *en* and *theos*, which together mean "God within." When we're grace-filled, there's no reason not to be both enthusiastic and grateful. Comparison's pessimism doesn't stand a chance when we view life this way.

If we turn to Scripture, Colossians 3:17 instructs us to give thanks no matter what we do. Granted, some circumstances may make this feel more like a chore than others. But the practice of gratitude can't be passive. It's not our default setting as humans—we're more apt to minimize, blame, and even deny the good in our lives. Even when it feels like everything is going wrong, we must retrain our brains to look for the good.

Corrie ten Boom was a Dutch Christian who endured months in a concentration camp during World War II after her family hid Jews. If anyone held reason for discontent, Corrie did. She lost her father and sister in the camps, and she unjustly endured humiliation and pain as a prisoner—all because she did something good.

But Corrie possessed a different attitude. She later published a book called *The Hiding Place*, which journaled her road to finding contentment in God through all she experienced. Here's how Corrie learned to find supernatural contentment: "If you look at the world, you'll be distressed. If you look within, you'll be depressed. If you look at God, you'll be at rest." That is a grace-filled life. And that, my friend, is where you find contentment.

Takeaway

In order to live a life free of comparison, we must live full of contentment. This requires us to examine and cut out our complaining, turn our hearts toward worship, and cultivate a heart of unending gratitude as we see life through the filter of grace.

Comparison-Free Life Action Plan

Read what the Bible has to say about contentment in the following passages: 2 Corinthians 5:15, Philippians 4:6–7, Hebrews 4:16, Hebrews 13:15, and Colossians 3:17. Write what you observe.

1. What are you most tempted to complain about? Are there areas in your life where it's more difficult to surrender to God's will or way? Do you ever find yourself wanting your own way? What can you do in these situations?

2. What helps you turn your heart toward worship? How could this help you crush comparison?

3. What does gratitude mean to you? What about contentment? Define these terms in your own words.

4. Can you think of anything you complained about that ultimately turned out to be an evidence of God's grace?

5. Start a gratitude journal. Write in it every day for the next fourteen days and try to start a habit of at least weekly journaling after that. What are you thankful for? Notice things both big and small. On hard days, it may be breath in your lungs or food on your table. Other days, you may be able to thank God for meeting personal needs or showing you his truth. Set a timer and try to write for at least three minutes every day. Share some of what you're grateful for with your group each week.

Memory Verse: "Rejoice always, pray without ceasing, give thanks in all circumstances; for this is the will of God in Christ Jesus for you" (1 Thess. 5:16–18).

Heavenly Father, please help me cut out complaining and see my life through the filter of grace. Bless my eyes to see the evidence of your grace everywhere I look, and remind me to be grateful and give thanks in all things. Amen.

Chapter Twelve

DISCOVER JOY

The very nature of Joy makes nonsense of our common distinction between having and wanting.

–C. S. Lewis

As I write this chapter, Marie Kondo's *Life-Changing Magic of Tidying Up* has become a Netflix sensation. Her book has already sold a bazillion copies, and after one episode of the show, my husband folds his shirts differently. If you missed this craze, let me tell you Marie's main thesis: Hug your stuff and see if it sparks joy. If it doesn't, get rid of it. Aside from the truth that, on most days, nothing in my closet sparks joy, it's a healthy exercise to evaluate our stuff from time to time. Stuff is the enemy of rest. We already have so much, and it seems the more we get, the more we need.

We're physically and emotionally burdened with stuff. We work more than we should so that we can have more than we need. We miss out on a lot of life to care for our stuff. Yet having "all the things" doesn't lead to contentment, joy, or rest. We carefully curate earthly treasures for our houses of sand, forgetting that someday it'll all be in someone's garage sale. Now, don't misunderstand me: this isn't about the quantity of our possessions. Minimalism can become an idol too. It's about the state of our hearts. When we put aside comparison's striving and hop off the "just a little more" (or minimalist "just a little less") treadmill, then we can rest.

To find more joy in our lives, we must first believe that we already have enough because of Jesus. Contentment begs us to recognize how grace and blessings—both seen and unseen—fill our lives. Having a heart of gratitude and practices like writing in a gratitude journal help us remember it. Likewise, joy takes its cues from gratitude. The joy-filled life is the thankful life.

Elsa Shirts and Grace

My husband, Eric, recently visited a Syrian refugee camp in Turkey. While he was there, he texted me pictures of the team handing out clothing and food. A little boy in one photo caught my eye. He wore a navy-blue T-shirt with Elsa (from the movie *Frozen*) on it. I thought about my boys. When they were younger, they would've screamed, fussed, and gone shirtless before donning Disney princess apparel. This little refugee boy didn't care about Elsa. He was grateful for the shirt.

What would it look like to thank God for the plain and obvious ways he's blessed us? What would it take to see the thousands of instances of God's grace in our everyday lives? Instead of seeing life's insufficiencies and lack, what if we tracked and expressed gratitude for all that we have?

My friend Kristi told me about a trip she took to the Dominican Republic to teach a women's conference there. While visiting one of the conference attendees in the woman's tiny, one-room home, Kristi's church team asked how they could pray for her. The woman's prayer? Please ask God to make me less materialistic. Wow!

It doesn't happen naturally. Our flesh is bent toward self-focus. Every day we must surrender and determine to walk in the Spirit. Galatians 5:22–23 tells us what that looks like: "But the fruit of the Spirit is love, joy, peace, patience, kindness, goodness, faithfulness, gentleness, self-control; against such things there is no law."

The Spirit-filled life isn't riddled with envy, covetousness, idolatry, and pride. It's comparison-free. It's thankful. It looks for evidence of grace every day, every hour. This is the key to unlocking your joy!

Defining Joy

During the first week of January, the staff at our new church engaged in a week of prayer and fasting. The topic: joy. But I felt joyless as the week began. The holidays were rough. My father-in-law received a terminal cancer diagnosis. This was our first year in a new place for Christmas, and I missed the familiarity of a calendar full of celebrations with friends. I felt sorry for myself. Poor me. Such a flood of grief consumed me on Christmas Eve, I decided to watch Hallmark Christmas movies and cry. (Pathetic, I know.)

A few weeks later, on day one of Joy Week, we were asked to take our "joy temperature." I knew mine hovered around freezing. I gave myself a 4 on a scale of 1 to 10. (That may have been generous, but I didn't feel like a total Scrooge.) After spending time in worship and hearing some great teaching on the topic, I started to feel my joy-o-meter rise. Then we were asked to write our own definitions of joy. Here's what I wrote: "Joy is the ever-available state of delight that comes with understanding who God is and who I am through him."

Though I've studied joy before and, intellectually, knew that joy didn't depend on circumstances, for the first time I realized that I could actually control the amount of joy I experienced. Joy isn't some elusive destination that's only accessible when life goes well. Joy is a state I can dwell in—at any time—through my connection with God. Did you catch that word *control*? For recovering perfectionists and chronic comparers like me, control is a constant battle. We want things to go our way, to puppeteer a life that feels safe and enjoyable. But this thought brings relief: though we can't control our circumstances, we *can* control how much joy we experience.

I was reminded of something else that's convicting: joy is not optional for the Christian. God's Word tells us hundreds of times in a variety of ways to rejoice in the Lord, shout for joy, and be glad! How's your joy level?[1] If you want to be joyful, you must practice joy. To be a violinist, you must practice with your bow on the strings. To be a writer, you must practice sitting still and putting words on the page. Athletes practice daily. Why should joy be any different?

There are three principles I believe help move us out of "I'll be happy when" land so we can relax on the sandy beaches of joy. Each pertains to the ways we relate to God, others, and ourselves.

Principle One: Jesus First

Growing up in church, there's one Sunday school song that pops into my head whenever I hear the word joy. The song uses joy as an acrostic for "Jesus and Others and You." The catchy tune serves a reminder to keep our priorities straight. I wish I could sing it for you. (Though you might not enjoy that!) Alas, reading will have to suffice for now. Here are the last few lines:

> "J" is for Jesus for He has first place,
> "O" is for others you meet face to face,
> "Y" is for you, in whatever you do,
> Put yourself third and spell JOY.[2]

For decades, I struggled with the mirror and the scale. I wrestled joy, in large part because of the nonstop conversation in my head focused on one important topic: me. What I looked like. What I ate that day. Whether or not I exercised. Whether or not my outfit looked cute enough. What did they think of me? What could I do to make them like me? Self-focus is exhausting.

Matthew 10:38–39 in *The Message* reads, "If you don't go all the way with me, through thick and thin, you don't deserve me. If your first concern is to look after yourself, you'll never find yourself. But if you forget about yourself and look to me, you'll find both yourself and me." That, my friends, is the freedom of self-forgetfulness.[3] This is the first secret to living a joy-filled life.

Between the Internet and our Fitbits, we're the most self-aware generation in history. But all this self-awareness has us scoring the highest levels of anxiety and depression ever recorded. It seems clear that the path to joy doesn't require me to keep a running tab of how I'm feeling every minute of every day. Joy comes when I can take my eyes off myself and fix my eyes on Jesus and the purpose he has for my life.

Joy percolates in my soul when my priority is to please God. How do we put Jesus first? We have to know him.

There's a chance that regularly engaging in spiritual disciplines—reading your Bible, praying, and engaging in your church community—may be a struggle. If comparison has consumed your life and joy seems like the wicked stepmother you'll never please, these practices may feel especially difficult.

Now, don't hear me wrong. We all go through seasons where aspects of our spiritual life feel stale. I've met some women who tell me that they read their Bibles every day but still can't stop comparing. I know others who feel like they pray all the time but still can't stop the running mental list of everything in their lives that could be better. We can't just pick and choose which spiritual disciplines we want to use. Actively engaging in all of them—to some extent—will help us truly experience the biblical kind of joy. Specifically, the disciplines of Bible study, prayer, fasting, confession, serving, giving, and community worship should regularly remind you to keep your eyes on Jesus and look through the lenses of grace.

If you need a place to start, reading the Bible daily will be a big help. The Center for Bible Engagement did a study and found that reading the Bible four times or more per week reduces loneliness by 30 percent, anger by 32 percent, and bitterness in relationships by 40 percent. That spiritually stagnant feeling? It goes away in 60 percent of those who read the Word regularly.[4] Psalm 19:8 tells us the precepts of the Lord bring joy to the heart. If your joy is low, read more!

If you're new to all this, regularly practicing spiritual disciplines won't feel easy. The devil will do whatever it takes to stop you from success. You'll sit down to pray, and a child will get stuck in the toilet. (It only happened once. Don't tell anyone.) Or, if you're alone, you'll suddenly notice the length of your toenails. I never notice my toenails until I try to pray. I attempt to stay focused, but the feeling in my toes grows stronger and stranger until I'm so overwhelmed by how weird my toenails feel, I must get up and clip them immediately. On my way back, I notice the load of laundry I meant to put in. I do that quickly. Then the phone rings. And, well, before I know it, my time for prayer is gone.

But I'm learning that—especially in busy seasons of our lives such as raising children or helping aging parents—prayer can be a daily conversation instead of a formal affair. Prayer needs to be more like that ever-running text thread with your best friend than your weekly meeting with your boss. This is important to understand because daily we are tempted to trust in what we see more than we trust in Jesus.

I signed up for Amazon Prime last month. (I know what you're thinking: welcome to the twenty-first century!) My hesitancy? Prime makes shopping too easy. Having anything I want or need come straight to my hands within forty-eight hours seemed dangerous for someone who loves shopping as much as I do. It turns out, I was right. Thanks to Amazon, I'm ordering posture-support devices (gotta correct that computer hump!), wool dryer balls (I didn't even know what they were last week!), and Larabars in flavors the stores don't sell (key lime pie, anyone?).

While I write this chapter on the left side of my screen, my web browser is peeking out from the right side and displaying a pair of sneakers I've been eyeing. Sadly, I'm wearing a pair of sneakers, and another older pair sits under my desk. But it *feels* like time for some new ones. After all, they're on sale. There are so many options. All delivered right to my door, anytime I determine I need it. My joy dissipates when I see all that I *could* have. I wonder: Does Prime affect more than just my wallet? Could it be that in my Amazon Prime world, I struggle even more with my prayer life?

I know Amazon has everything I need. I have complete faith that they'll get it to me in forty-eight hours. (Or, if they mess up, they'll give me a refund!) But God? Often he's not that predictable. What if I ask for something he doesn't want me to have? I'll sit by the door waiting for his van to come, but I'll never see it. Prayer requires me to have faith that God will deliver if and when he deems it right.

Does it sometimes feel easier to have faith in Amazon? Our have-it-in-an-instant culture makes it even harder to pray and believe that God will provide for our needs. So we avoid prayer. Maybe we feel our prayers are too selfish or too trivial for God to notice. I tend to fret over whether or not I followed the right "prayer formula" or spent the proper amount of time praising God before making my requests known. But God just wants us to pray.

He wants us to ask. In fact, John 16:24 seems to imply that unless we're asking God for what we desire, we'll never have fullness of joy. It reads, "Until now you have asked nothing in my name. Ask, and you will receive, that your joy may be full."

Prayer and joy are inexplicably connected because God is the source of all of our joy. Psalm 16:11 says, "You make known to me the path of life; in your presence there is fullness of joy; at your right hand are pleasures forevermore." Connection to him brings true satisfaction for our longings. No connection equals no contentment. Living the life of grace means we can stop plotting for our best life now and instead ask God for what we want—confident that he's not just looking out for us, but he seeks our delight!

To live the life of grace, we have to know and be connected to our power source. Your cell phone battery will not last unless you charge it regularly. Energy only comes when we're connected to the power. Matthew 5:14 tells us that we are the light of the world. Yet too often we try to muster up enough energy on our own to shine. Comparison feeds our futility by telling us we're not shining bright enough. *You need more light! Just a little brighter . . . then you'll have it.*

Friend, we have an unlimited power source. He always gives us the fuel we need to burn bright. We must choose to be plugged in. When I try to go on my own power, I surge and flicker. I tire and burn out. I'm a dying cell phone with no charger in sight. But God offers a constant source of abundant energy. Nehemiah 8:10 explains that "the joy of the LORD is your strength." Without joy, we're lusterless weaklings.

Note: Paul Miller's book *A Praying Life* has done more to transform my view of prayer than forty years in church combined. If you struggle in this area, I highly recommend it.

Principle Two: Love and Know Others

Back to my Sunday school song: Jesus and others and you. We've talked about Jesus and how to connect with him, but what about loving and serving others? The truth is we can't live a comparison-free life without other people in it.

There are a few reasons "knowing people" can be helpful for living a comparison-free life. First of all, Jesus commands it. Seriously, friends, if Jesus decided he needed twelve guys to do life with, who do we think we are trying to do it alone? No, our Facebook friends don't count. We need people for both accountability and encouragement. Hebrews 10:24 tells us to "spur one another" toward love and good deeds (NLT), while Ecclesiastes 4:9–12 tells us that friends are important for sharing our hurts and pain.

Science agrees. A meta-analysis of 148 scientific studies showed that good relationships keep us happier and healthier. Interestingly enough, the opposite is also true. A lack of social relationships puts someone at greater risk for poor health than cigarette smoking, obesity, and high blood pressure. You have a 50 percent increased likelihood of survival if you have strong social relationships.[5]

That's just the data on knowing people and having good friends. When we help others, we experience greater joy and happiness and feel our lives have more meaning. Furthermore, expressing gratitude to others—as assessed by one study where participants wrote gratitude letters to someone who had positively impacted their lives—also leads people to feel like their lives have even greater meaning.[6]

And, check this out. Science tells us that becoming friends with those people with whom you tend to compare yourself changes the way you think—not just about them, but about yourself. As we've already established, comparison colors how you see the world. When we compete with each other, we tend to see others and ourselves more negatively. But when researchers put former competitors into situations where they needed to cooperate (i.e., on the same team in a game or project), study participants had more positive thoughts about both themselves and their former rivals.[7]

The science is clear on the benefit of in-person relationships, but in real life, they seem to be getting more difficult to sustain. A few decades ago, relating to people felt different. Relationships were still difficult, friendships were awkward at the start, but connection was clearer. It didn't happen unless you were in the same room or both holding a telephone to your ears. Phones rang in our dorm rooms, not on our person. If you weren't in your room, you missed the call. Hopefully, your answering machine worked, so at least you would know what you missed. If I wanted to see someone in particular, I couldn't use Facebook; I figured out their class schedule and tried to intercept them on their way back to their dorm or into the cafeteria.

Now, relationships feel more confusing, and I believe this impacts our joy in significant ways. Our lack of connection feeds our comparison issues a steady stream of "everyone out there is better off than me." To answer that lie, there's no substitute for actually knowing and relating to other people. And, in order to do that well, you may have to take a break from social media.

I understand what I'm asking. Taking Facebook off your phone may feel like you're moving into a bunker to wait out the war. But if comparison is your drug, social media is your dealer. Don't think you're addicted? Studies show the urge to check social media accounts is stronger than the urge for sex. To get free, you may need to spend some time in rehab.[8]

Social media offers us a fake sense of connection. Studies have proven that when friends press "like" or we see an informative status update, we experience a false bond. We get a hit of dopamine, but only enough to make us crave more responses and keep us addicted. Compulsive Internet users are lonelier, are more depressed, and exhibit poorer social skills than those who do not spend too much time online. Studies also show that the overuse of social networking sites has significant negative consequences on all aspects of one's well-being.[9]

The truth is, you don't need a bunch of scientific data to convince you. You probably already know that having coffee with a friend feels different than an hour on Instagram. Chances are, you already recognize how time spent in meaningful conversation helps you feel better about your life and less likely to compare, while that same time spent on Facebook escorts you directly to comparison's prison cell. The question is, Will you do something about it?

Those Facebook and Instagram "stories"? They're no substitute for sitting with a friend and sharing yours. Telling your story, according to neuroscience, actually synchronizes our brains. It helps us understand each other better, empathize, and connect.[10] My friend, author Christine Hoover, explains one genius reason why our social media relationships are no substitute for real ones: We are embodied people! Though we believe we can equally engage in both virtual relationships and real-live ones, something strange happens when we lose sight of our physical limits. Christine explains, "We believe God is asking us to carry every concern and speak about every piece of news . . . we start to believe we're godlike."[11]

Honestly ask yourself this question: Has time on social media ever overwhelmed you with joy? Probably not. Epicurus once wrote, "Do not spoil what you have by desiring what you have not; but remember that what you now have was once among the things only hoped for." Real relationships give us an appreciation for what we have—compassion and gratitude for other people—while social media leaves us hungry for more of what this earth offers—be it power, influence, or better stuff. Friend, I want to see you free from comparison. But, realistically, your freedom may cost you some time online.

Principle Three: The New You

You may have been excited to get to the "you" portion of my J-O-Y acrostic. *Yay!* You may be thinking: *finally, she's going to tell me how to love myself.* But friend, I'm not. Here's why. As I read my Bible, I see we have but two great commands: to love Jesus, then to love others (John 13:34; Mark 12:31). We don't have to increase our love for ourselves. Matthew 22:39 implies that we already have enough self-love. Instead, we are instructed to love others as we *already* love ourselves. We don't have to love our lives. (John 12:25 states just the opposite.) We don't need more self-love. (2 Timothy 3:2 warns how in the last days, men will be lovers of self, and it's not a good thing!) Neither do we need to love ourselves before we can love others. If this were the case, then there would be three great commands, when Matthew 22:40 only counts two.

We don't have to love our homes, wardrobes, or thighs. In fact, our best chance at living comparison-free comes not when we love ourselves or our lives, but when we can surrender all of our earthly loves for the ultimate better: Jesus. An old hymn crystalizes this truth. Written by Helen Howarth Lemmel in 1922, the chorus goes like this: "Turn your eyes upon Jesus, Look full in his wonderful face. And the things of earth will grow strangely dim, in the light of his glory and grace."[12]

The life of comparison is the old nature, not the new nature. Now, through grace, we have a fresh way of viewing the world. We are dead to our old ways of thinking and living. In Ephesians 4:24, Paul instructs, "Put on the new self, created after the likeness of

God in true righteousness and holiness." This truth, my friend, is why there's nothing stopping you from living comparison-free. Joy awaits those who are willing to keep their eyes fixed on heaven.

Strengthen your relationship with Jesus. Love and engage in real relationships with others. Rely on Christ alone for your contentment and on his grace for your identity. Practice gratitude every day. Instead of chasing those "ers" (better, thinner, healthier, nicer, happier) to win comparison battles, surrender the burden of comparison and receive the goodness of grace.

My mom quotes Psalm 30:5 all the time: "Weeping may last through the night, but joy comes with the morning" (NLT). Further down in the passage, David talks about how the Lord has turned his mourning into joyful dancing and clothed him in gladness. (Seems like an outfit that would pass the Marie Kondo test!) Today, I notice something else in this passage. David played an active role in his journey to joy. He sang to the Lord. He praised his name. He acknowledged God's favor and exalted the Lord. David worshipped actively!

Christianity is the only religion in the world that doesn't require you to "do" more. The work (Jesus's death on the cross) is already done.[13] Like we discussed in an earlier chapter, you don't have to "work" for it. Though trying to earn grace is futile, actively engaging in practices to help you stay comparison-free and grace-filled is essential! When you're tempted to compare, immerse yourself in activities that strengthen your faith. Instead of writing (yet another) list of self-improvement tasks, determine to study a book of the Bible or to learn the memory verses at the end of each of these chapters. God doesn't want us to be lazy, but pursuing our earthly goals apart from seeking first his kingdom always leads to futility.

Do you crave more joy? Do you want to have the strength to resist when the temptation to compare comes? Get active. Are you ready to lay down the burden of comparison and enjoy a grace-filled, joy-filled life? The formula is as simple as this: Seek him. Praise him. Thank him.

Takeaway

Joy is a mandate for the Christian life. Living comparison-free and grace-filled can help spark joy in our hearts as we remember to keep our J-O-Y (Jesus and others and you) priorities rightly ordered. We can experience firsthand how the joy of the Lord is our strength when we seek him, praise him, and thank him.

Comparison-Free Life Action Plan

What can you learn about joy from the following verses? See James 1:2–3, Psalm 47:1, Ecclesiastes 9:7, Proverbs 10:28, 1 Peter 1:8–9, Romans 15:13, and Nehemiah 8:10.

1. On a scale of 1 to 10 (with 10 being the top), what is your joy level? Would you like to increase it? From what you've just read, what are some ways you could turn to Jesus for a joy boost this week?

2. How's your prayer life? Are you reading the Bible regularly? What do you think of the concept that unless we are plugged in, we have no power?

3. How do you think our Amazon Prime, have-it-in-an-instant culture affects the way we interact with God? Has this impacted you too?

4. Does social media help you experience more joy or comparison? How grateful do you feel while scrolling? Would a week or two off your social media accounts help you?

5. What are you doing to turn your heart toward worship and away from envy, covetousness, jealousy, and pride?

Memory Verse: "And do not be grieved, for the joy of the Lord is your strength" (Neh. 8:10b).

Heavenly Father, increase my joy and give me strength. Show me how to apply the principles of rightly ordered priorities—Jesus and others before self. Help me walk in the Spirit and find contentment in order to experience true joy. Amen.

Conclusion

DISCOVER REST

Our heart is not quiet until it rests in thee.

–Augustine, *Confessions*

Can I confess something? I don't know when to quit.

I feel as if I always could do a little bit more. Finishing this book is no exception. Yesterday, for example, I finished everything I absolutely needed to accomplish for the day by eleven A.M. I should have quit. I should have stopped and done something fun with my children or folded the laundry. Instead, I kept going. The voice in my head teased me with this lie: "Wouldn't you feel even better if you got even *more* done?" So I kept working. At three P.M., I sat at my desk. Still working. Still listening to that prompt, "Just a little more. Then you'll be there. Then you'll be far enough ahead. Then you will be able to relax."

In anticipation of an upcoming busy season in our lives, I've been working for the past two weeks to get "ahead." I've made twelve freezer meals. I've cleaned my house so I'm ready to neglect it for a few weeks. I've washed sheets and rugs, organized, decluttered. Yet it feels like I'm stuck in "go" mode. Every ounce of work I do to get ahead never feels like enough. There's always one more task to be completed that "should" have been on the list.

Why do I work so hard? The voice in my head says if I keep on working, then I'll be able to rest. Rest is the temptation that lures me, yet I'm barely conscious of the vigilance with which I chase it.

My friend Jena Morrow Margis wrote a tremendous memoir called *Hollow.* It's her very personal story of a severe battle with anorexia. In it, she details the way the anorexic thinks. "Just a few more pounds . . . then you'll be there." The voices that drive extreme weight loss and destructive eating behaviors taunt so many. It's the same lie comparison tells. If we could just get a little more, do a little more, work a little harder . . . then we'll get there. Then we can stop striving and relax. The deceiver of our souls knows that rest is a reward for which we'll work.

But then there's grace. Grace says we don't have to earn our rest. Jesus already paid for it. Think about it: Does the rich man ever have "enough" money? Can the perfectionist ever make life perfect "enough"? Can I ever get far "enough" ahead in my writing, housework, or cooking? The answer is no. We strive for an earthly "enough" that never arrives. If we look for rest in achievements, stuff, and checked-off to-do lists, it will ever elude us. Hebrews 13:5–6 instructs:

> Keep your life free from love of money, and be content with what you have, for he has said, "I will never leave you nor forsake you." So we can confidently say, "The Lord is my helper; I will not fear; what can man do to me?"

Because Jesus is our helper, because he will never leave us or forsake us, we can be content. Because he is always with us, we have no reason to fear. When I can stop striving for more and stop fearing the opinions of others (and my own opinions of myself), I am truly able to rest.

Today, on Facebook, I noted a great irony. A friend posted, "What's the greatest compliment you could receive?" She quickly had sixty-five comments and counting. Not one response focused on physical appearance, being great at a job, or having amazing possessions. Instead, those who commented shared a desire for compliments about their faithfulness, their impact on others, and their obvious love for family and friends. I know this may not be a representative sample, but I find it peculiar how much time we spend working hard at things that don't really matter, even to us! Truly all of our work is in vain unless we're submitted to God's plan for our lives. No amount of work will lead me to a place of ultimate contentment. No amount of work will ever yield the rest I crave. Grace and gratitude are my only ticket out of comparison land. They are my only chance to find some semblance of peace here on earth.

Ultimate Rest

Today my family faces a sad reality. Just yesterday, the doctor told my father-in-law his cancer is no longer treatable. He was given a few weeks to live. He'll be gone long before anyone reads this book.

Last month, my aunt passed away, just twenty-eight days after her cancer diagnosis. With aging parents and grandparents nearing the centurion point, I've wondered how many funerals we'll have to attend over the next few years.

Death has a distinct way of reminding us about what's really important in life, doesn't it? Weeks ago, I sat on the floor of my late-aunt's home, rummaging under her bed like a burglar on a mission. Her safe was hidden, and we needed it to find her important documents. We searched closets and dumped out drawers, and as we did, we created a very chaotic mess of her stuff. Everywhere.

She'd taken nothing with her. It was all still there, in her home—everything, including her breakfast dishes—just as she left it. As my aunt sat in the hospital bed, days before her death, my mom asked, "Can we bring you anything from home?" Aunt Pam whispered no. For where she was going, all she needed was Jesus.

Our stuff becomes increasingly meaningless as we near the end of life, doesn't it? So do our selfish ambitions and fleshly desires. I've never heard of a person who died disappointed that they didn't lose another twenty pounds so they'd look better in their casket. If we knew we only had a few weeks or months to live, would we spend that time dieting, working overtime, and remodeling our bathrooms? Or would we develop a new appreciation for what we have and who we share it with?

Aunt Pam died with a smile on her face. I know it's because she was going to meet Jesus. She caught a glimpse of heaven and beamed, knowing that even more awaited her. That's true rest. I wonder if God's desire isn't for us all to have that same knowing smile long before we reach our deathbeds. I wonder if he doesn't long for us to find his joy, peace, and rest while we walk among the living.

I believe it's possible. The person who receives the terminal diagnosis no longer feels encumbered by all of life's demands. She doesn't worry about wearing Michael Kors or driving a Lincoln. She's inoculated from even the most effective advertising campaigns that tell her she needs to get toned or rich. Instead, she's free to think of life in light of eternity.

But here's the craziest thing, friend: through Jesus, we are too. The degree to which we're able to see Jesus is the degree to which we'll be able to find rest. We don't have to be slaves to culture's expectations. Jesus tells us over and again in the New Testament that we don't have to live like everyone else.

Where's My Worship?

Remember the irony of the scenario I described in this book's introduction? I stood in a worship service singing praise to God while secretly comparing myself to other worshippers. Though my actions—standing and singing—may have made it seem, outwardly, like I was worshipping God, my focus was really on myself.

If we truly desire rest, we must be constantly aware of what it is we're worshipping. When I compare, I worship my ideals, my idols, or myself. To truly live comparison-free, I must keep my focus—my reverence and adoration—on the God who is beyond all compare. Ultimately, all of our comparison issues are about misplaced worship. The stress of comparison melts away when I recognize this truth and determinedly set aside all that distracts me and demands my admiration. As Mark Labberton says in his book, *The Dangerous Idea of Worship*, "Worship sets us free from ourselves to be free for God and God's purposes."[1]

Freedom, rest, contentment, peace, and joy . . . they all require but one thing of us—that we be mindful of who and what we worship. The burden of comparison lifts when the melody of our hearts shifts from "What about me?" to "I stand in awe of you."

Choose Where You're Going

Last night my middle son, Trevor, saw a commercial that referenced baseball as America's game. He asked, "Why is baseball America's game? Whose game is soccer?"

"Probably Europe," I answer.

"Why can't I be from Europe?" he responds.

"Because you're from Texas. You can't choose where you're from; you can only choose where you're going."

If your life has been characterized by comparison, today's a new day. God gives you the chance to start again, fresh. That's what grace is all about. You can't go back—you can't rewrite the story you've already lived—but you can choose where you're headed. You can determine to have a comparison-free, grace- and gratitude-filled future. You don't have to compare because it's an instinct; you've been given the spirit of self-control to help in every situation where the flesh wants to rule.

I will only be content in his grace. I can rest, truly rest, when I remember that the work has already been finished. If God could take care of my sin problem, there's nothing else in my life he can't handle. Nothing else is sufficient. That's what comparison-free living is all about.

When I do anything like my life depends on it, I do it as an idolater. I trade my identity as a worshipper for a cheap substitute. I believe my body size, bank account, business card, or farmhouse kitchen will solidify my identity. These first-world goals never satisfy. My life depends on Jesus alone. He's all I'll have at the end. He's all I truly have every day. These other things, identities, successes—I can't take them with me.

That drive that makes you want to do better, win the race, make a difference—God put that there for him to use. He has gifted and empowered you and given you the grace to do amazing work for his kingdom—not for self-gain. Unlike winning the beauty contest, living in the perfect home, or being the "best" in whatever area you deem important today, when you put all that energy and drive into working for Jesus, you *can* take it with you. Fan the flame of your purpose. Store up your treasure in heaven. And then, my friend, you'll discover the joy of comparison-free life.

NOTES

Chapter One: Sweating All Stuff

[1] Thomas McMullan, "This Is What Jealousy Does to the Brain," Alphr, October 18, 2017, www.alphr.com/bioscience/1007405/this-is-what-jealousy-does-to-the-brain/.

Chapter Two: Wanted–A Better Life

[1] Philip Brickman, Dan Coates, and Ronnie Janoff-Bulman, "Lottery Winners and Accident Victims: Is Happiness Relative?" *Journal of Personality and Social Psychology* 36, no. 8 (1978): 917–27.

[2] Saul Levine, "What Makes a Worthy Person? 'The Four B's,'" *Psychology Today*, March 8, 2016, www.psychologytoday.com/us/blog/our-emotional-footprint/201603/what-makes-worthy-person-the-four-bs/.

Chapter Three: Comparison's Con

[1] "Leon Festingers's Social Comparison Theory," The Psychology Notes HQ, March 10, 2018, www.psychologynoteshq.com/leonfestinger-socialcomparisontheory/.

[2] Press Release, "Comparing Yourself to Others Can Have Health Impacts," Penn State News, February 7, 2012, https://news.psu.edu/story/151929/2012/02/07/comparing-yourself-others-can-have-health-impacts.

[3] Theodore A. Powers, Richard Koestner, and David C. Zuroff, "Self-Criticism, Goal Motivation, and Goal Progress," *Journal of Social and Clinical Psychology* 27, no. 7 (2007): 826–40.

[4] Sonja Lyubomirsky, *The How of Happiness: A Scientific Approach to Getting the Life You Want* (New York: Penguin, 2007), 98–99.

[5] Juliana Breines, "The Perils of Comparing Ourselves to Others," *Psychology Today*, July 31, 2016, www.psychologytoday.com/us/blog/in-love-and-war/201607/the-perils-comparing-ourselves-others.

[6] Helmut Apel, Jan Crusius, and Alexander L. Gerlach, "Social Comparison, Envy, and Depression on Facebook: A Study Looking at the Effects of High Comparison Standards on Depressed Individuals," *Journal of Social and*

Clinical Psychology 34, no. 4 (December 2015): 277–89, www.researchgate.net/publication/274067560_Social_Comparison_Envy_and_Depression_on_Facebook_A_Study_Looking_at_the_Effects_of_High_Comparison_Standards_on_Depressed_Individuals.

Chapter Four: Escaping the Trap

[1] Robert M. Pirsig, *Zen and the Art of Motorcycle Maintenance* (New York: William Morrow and Company, 1974).

[2] Richard Smith, "What Is the Difference between Envy and Jealousy?" *Psychology Today*, January 3, 2014, www.psychologytoday.com/us/blog/joy-and-pain/201401/what-is-the-difference-between-envy-and-jealousy.

[3] Richard Smith, "The Important Distinction between Benign and Malicious Envy," *Psychology Today*, January 11, 2015, www.psychologytoday.com/us/blog/joy-and-pain/201501/the-important-distinction-between-benign-and-malicious-envy.

[4] Smith, "The Important Distinction between Benign and Malicious Envy."

[5] C. S. Lewis, *Mere Christianity* (London: MacMillan, 1978), 109, 110.

Chapter Five: The Ideal Me

[1] Timothy J. Keller, *Counterfeit Gods: The Empty Promises of Money, Sex, and Power, and the Only Hope That Matters* (New York: Penguin Books, 2011), xx.

Chapter Six: Accepted and Approved

[1] Jeremy Treat, "Grace Is Not a Thing," The Gospel Coalition, May 29, 2019, www.thegospelcoalition.org/article/grace-is-not-a-thing/.

[2] Max Lucado, *Grace: More Than We Deserve, Greater Than We Imagine* (Nashville: Thomas Nelson, 2014), 83.

[3] Max Lucado, *Wild Grace: What Happens When Grace Happens* (Nashville: Thomas Nelson, 2012), 141.

[4] Heather Holleman, *Seated with Christ: Living Freely in a Culture of Comparison* (Chicago: Moody, 2015). These concepts are explored in chapters 3 through 5.

Chapter Seven: Grace Alleviates Our Fears

[1] Stephen Covey, *The 7 Habits of Highly Effective People* (New York: Simon & Schuster, 2013), 219, 298.

Chapter Eight: God Gives Great Makeovers

[1] Paul David Tripp, "Wednesday's Word: Thanking God," PaulTripp.com, www.paultripp.com/ViewMail.aspx?p=858F5c1501009858F5cF6&mmid=F555G345143F555G3eB.

[2] Stephen Altrogge, *The Greener Grass Conspiracy: Finding Contentment on Your Side of the Fence* (Wheaton, IL: Crossway, 2011), 63.

Chapter Nine: Life Is Bigger than Me

[1] Timothy J. Keller, former pastor of Redeemer Presbyterian Church in New York, has many sermons available here: www.gospelinlife.com/free-sermon-resource.

[2] Timothy Lane and Paul David Tripp, *How People Change* (Greensboro, NC: New Growth Press, 2008), 15.

Chapter Ten: Don't Miss the Party

[1] Timothy J. Keller, *Reason for God: Belief in an Age of Skepticism* (New York: Penguin, 2008), 25.

[2] Kyle Idelman, *Grace Is Greater: God's Plan to Overcome Your Past, Redeem Your Pain, and Rewrite Your Story* (Grand Rapids, MI: Baker Books, 2018), 70.

Chapter Eleven: Discover Contentment

[1] Travis Bradberry, "How Complaining Rewires Your Brain for Negativity," *Talentsmart Newsletter*, www.talentsmart.com/articles/How-Complaining-Rewires-Your-Brain-for-Negativity-2147446676-p-1.html.

[2] Alex Korb, "The Grateful Brain," *Psychology Today*, November 20, 2012, www.psychologytoday.com/us/blog/prefrontal-nudity/201211/the-grateful-brain.

Chapter Twelve: Discover Joy

[1] David Mathis, "Joy Is Not Optional: Why Your Happiness Matters to God," DesiringGod.org, February 3, 2016, www.desiringgod.org/articles/joy-is-not-optional.

[2] B. Metzger, "Jesus and Others and You," 1951.

[3] Timothy J. Keller, *The Freedom of Self-Forgetfulness: The Path to True Christian Joy* (La Grange, KY: 10 Publishing, 2012), is an amazing resource for learning this principle.

[4] "Research," Back to the Bible, accessed April 2, 2020, www.backtothebible.org/research.

[5] Julianne Holt-Lunstad, Timothy B. Smith, and J. Bradley Layton, "Social Relationships and Mortality Risk: A Meta-Analytic Review," *PLoS Med* 7, no. 7 (July 27, 2010): https://doi.org/10.1371/journal.pmed.1000316.

[6] Benjamin P. Hardy, "This 75-year Harvard Study Shows How to Have a Lifetime of Joy," The Ladders, May 1, 2018, www.theladders.com/career-advice/this-75-year-harvard-study-shows-how-to-have-lifetime-joy. The original study is available at www.adultdevelopmentstudy.org/grantandglueckstudy.

[7] Elizabeth Hopper, "Can Helping Others Help You Find Meaning in Life?" *Greater Good Magazine*, February 16, 2016, https://greatergood.berkeley.edu/article/item/can_helping_others_help_you_find_meaning_in_life.

[8] Daryl Nelson, "Study: Checking Your Social Media Page Is as Addictive as Sex and Nicotine," Consumer Affairs, October 5, 2012, www.consumeraffairs.com/news04/2012/10/study-checking-your-social-media-pages-is-as-addictive-as-sex-and-nicotine.html.

[9] Spencer Palmer Christensen, "Social Media Use and Its Impact on Relationships and Emotions" (master's thesis, Brigham Young University, 2018), 10, https://scholarsarchive.byu.edu/cgi/viewcontent.cgi?article=7927&context=etd.

[10] Joshua Gowin, "Why Sharing Stories Brings People Together," *Psychology Today*, June 6, 2011, www.psychologytoday.com/us/blog/you-illuminated/201106/why-sharing-stories-brings-people-together.

[11] Christine Hoover, *With All Your Heart: Living Joyfully through Allegiance to King Jesus* (Grand Rapids, MI: Baker Books, 2020), 127.

[12] Helen Howarth Lemmel, "Turn Your Eyes Upon Jesus," 1922. Lyrics accessed at www.hymnary.org.

[13] "Do vs. Done" is an illustration used by Campus Crusade for Christ International (CRU) to teach the gospel. It can be found at www.cru.org/content/dam/cru/legacy/2012/01/dovsdone.pdf.

Conclusion: Discover Rest

[1] Mark Labberton, *The Dangerous Act of Worship: Living God's Call to Justice* (Downers Grove, IL: InterVarsity Press, 2014), 14.